IS YOUR

MARRIAGE

REALLY WORTH
FIGHTING FOR?

JAY KESLER

WITH JOE MUSSER

IS YOUR

MARRIAGE

REALLY WORTH
FIGHTING FOR?

LIFEJOURNEY
BOOKS

David C. Cook Publishing Co.
Elgin, Illinois - Weston, Ontario

121373

LifeJourney Books is an imprint of David C. Cook Publishing Co.
David C. Cook Publishing Co., Elgin, Illinois 60120
David C. Cook Publishing Co., Weston, Ontario

IS YOUR MARRIAGE REALLY WORTH FIGHTING FOR?

Cover and interior design by Bill Paetzold

First Printing, 1989
Printed in the United States of America
93 92 91 90 89 5 4 3 2 1

Unless otherwise noted, Scripture is taken from the HOLY BIBLE, NEW
INTERNATIONAL VERSION (NIV). Copyright © 1973, 1978, 1984
International Bible Society. Used by permission of Zondervan Bible
Publishers.

Kesler, Jay
        Is Your Marriage Really Worth Fighting For? / by Jay Kesler with
            Joe Musser.
                    p.   cm.
        "LifeJourney Books."
        ISBN 1-55513-259-6
        1. Marriage.   I. Musser, Joe. II. Title.
        HQ734.K423   1989
        646.7´8—dc20   89-34266
                                        CIP

CONTENTS

Introduction   9

1 Don't Think 'Too Late' Too Soon   19

2 The Source of Our Pain   33

3 Feelings Follow Actions   51

4 Love Is Forgiving   65

5 Expectations and Misconceptions   79

6 Male and Female Differences   89

7 Maturity Is Not Monotony   99

8 The Courtship Restored   109

9 The Rediscovery Process   125

10 A New Intimacy: Two Shall Become One   137

Introduction

I host a radio program called "Family Forum," and some time ago one of the producers reminded me that the broadcast is heard 68,000 times a year somewhere in the United States, Caribbean, or Europe. In response to the program, we receive lots of mail. And I realize that the many thousands of responses to our radio exposure has affected the way I think about marriage—especially marriage within a Christian context.

I am reminded of the phrase that Leo Tolstoy used in the introduction to his classic novel, *Anna Karenina*. He states that all happy families are very much alike and, conversely, all unhappy families are similar in their own sad way. There are many unhappy stories in the world and, frankly, most of them are too involved for us to even begin to tell.

People often ask me if we make up the questions used on the broadcast. I confess that we don't, but that we often have to edit them very heavily because of the depth of heartaches that pour from the letters. The writers share details that are too personal, too revealing, and too involved to read on the air.

What I detect is a sense of universal concern—a certain sameness. Many people who have committed their lives to Jesus Christ, who would answer immediately and forthrightly that they are Christians, are struggling within their marriages. But rather than relate to their marriage problems from a Christian world view, their responses are the same as non-Christians who have never even begun to think about the Gospel. They are giving in to the same influences and for the same reasons.

This book is not about marriage in the broadest sense or even about Christian marriage. It's for those who are struggling with their marriages—those sad souls who are living with a "low-grade fever" within what they once hoped would be happiness and bliss. This book is written for people who really don't want to give up on their crumbling marriages, and who are willing to "give it a try" within the context of uniquely Christian teachings and principles. We have God's promise in I John 4:4: "The One who is in you is greater than the one who is in the world." For this reason alone, it would seem that Christians should not be giving in to the same forces and pressures so common within the institution of marriage today.

This book is for married people who are so desperate to save their marriage that they might actually reconsider applying Christian faith and principles to their situation. They might even be willing to realistically consider the vows which were made at the marriage altar—including that frightening phrase, "Till death do us part."

A HIGHER POWER IS AVAILABLE

I have assumed in the writing of this book that a Christian has a higher power available within his or her life. I am not referring just to the Holy Spirit who empowers the believer, but also to the sense that God's teachings themselves have the power to correct flaws and to reorient life. This unusual power available to Christians can help us reestablish good relationships. But such power is not available to a person who does not take the Christian faith seriously.

So this book is for Christians who believe that the God who created the world has also created them. We who believe that the Creator *made us* should also be convinced that He knows how to *fix us*. The Lord God has revealed Himself in the Bible. The Scriptures tell us about *relationships*—between God and man, and between man and his fellow man. Marriage is certainly about relationships, so all the relational promises in the Bible are available to Christians within marriage. The same principles that apply to general relationships are just as valid for the fractured relationships in marriage.

I must confess that this book has a two-pronged bias. One bias is that the Christian message is unique, powerful, and strong. It goes beyond creed or belief, and will really make a difference in our lives. The other bias is that it is possible for two people to make a marriage work if they are willing to make the effort. This book encourages us not to give up so easily.

Many Christians, including Christian leaders, believe that divorce is inevitable even among believers. Statistics for marriage breakup in the church follow the same general curve as the secular public. As a result, we have become brainwashed by the secularists and humanists to believe that our Christian faith is really irrelevant in regard to such discouraging trends.

Actually, the statistics *are* on the side of the pessimist. Dr. James Dobson says that the number of Christians who get divorced is not much different than the statistics for secular society. There is truly very little difference in the actual numbers.

This is not exactly fresh news. Almost any periodical printed today will have an article on the breakdown of the family. In fact, the societal concerns are varied and profound. The issue of family breakups can be approached in a number of ways: children born out of wedlock, problems with the welfare system, aid to dependent children, social problems of promiscuity, the dreaded presence of AIDS in our culture, "latchkey children," single-parent families, injustice in compensation between males and females in the workplace that cause working mothers such stress, and so forth.

Growing concern in these (and a thousand other areas) cause great debates within our society. They rightfully take up the time of social service counselors, those in other helping professions, and vast numbers of government agencies.

But I believe this bombardment of the family by the enemy is not sociological or societal. Rather, it is a *theological* battle. After reading all the mail I have received, I have come to the conclusion that Christian marriages are the focal point of the enemy's attack. From a strategic viewpoint, we need to accept the premise that the devil is "like a roaring lion walking about seeking whomever he can devour." It shouldn't surprise us that Satan's attack is on the family, and specifically where male and female come together in marriage.

WHEN FAMILY RELATIONSHIPS BREAK DOWN

From Genesis to Revelation, God's relationship to mankind is consistently described in terms of a family illustration. God is a father; we are His children. We are sons and daughters, brothers and sisters. The Lord Jesus Christ is the Bridegroom; we are the bride. It is terribly sad that these illustrations and relationships are increasingly losing their meanings.

I suppose this became most evident to me when I was working with young people within Youth for Christ. The family casualties and problems were especially visible when working with inner-city youths and within the juvenile justice system. We would take kids away to camp for a week or two to give them some sense of love and normalcy away from their hostile environment. We fed them all the food they could eat and brought in a bright, enthusiastic, upbeat Christian staff to work with them. We treated them to all sorts of enjoyable activities.

Soon we saw a level of trust start to develop. A deep bond of affection between staff and kids started to grow, and the groundwork began for planting the Christian Gospel. Yet because most of us were trained in conventional methods of communication and had been raised in "normal" homes and families, we presented the Gospel in terms of our own understanding. We would say things such as, "God is your heavenly Father," intended to invoke feelings of security, protection, nurture, provision, happiness, contentment, and thoughts of a loving and caring Provider. Our typical idea of "father" was intended to break down barriers and develop trust.

The problem was, it often had the *opposite* effect. As we used these terms with the kids, they would tense up and get a glazed-over look in their eyes. Eventually it dawned on us what was happening. These kids were from hurting families. The references to family that provided us with warm feelings of well-being were conjuring up a sense of panic for them!

What did these kids think about when someone said "Father"? Maybe someone who comes home late at night, involved in all sorts of sinful, capricious, and arbitrary behavior. Perhaps someone who was constantly drunk, or even abusive. "Father" may be someone who kicks you down the stairs, breaks an end table over your head, swears till three in the morning, and vomits all over the kitchen table.

Without even realizing it, we started those kids thinking, *These people have brought me away to camp where I can get some relief from that no-good (expletive) who calls himself my father, and now they are telling me what I need is a great big one of these! No way!*

The situation grew worse as we told them their heavenly Father is omnipresent, all-powerful, and knows everything that is going on. The kids' warped concept of "father" combined with God's omnipotent attributes was an absolute turnoff to them. It became evident to us that we had to have some other ideas and role models before we could work effectively with them.

The same may be true as we tackle the subject of Christian marriage and helping people to begin to solve their problems. We can't begin to unravel the twisted turmoil of problems resulting from sexual child abuse, psychological trauma, or other difficult and "impossible" situations. Yet we need to be aware that they exist and affect many of today's marriages. To ignore these and other problems in Christian marriage simply adds to the long list of social issues with which we are threatened.

Threatened marriages carry a deeper concern of alienation from God. As we discuss the relationship of man and wife to be a reflection of the relationship of Christ (the bridegroom) and His church (the bride), it's not hard to see that the idea will be unwelcome, capricious, and arbitrary to many people. A hostile or abusive husband is one in which no woman can put her eternal trust. So to talk about Jesus Christ as Bridegroom is futile.

I have concluded that the enemy attacks Christian marriage for far deeper reasons than to further burden people who already have plenty of problems. Satan's primary attack is at the point where man and woman come together in a Christian marriage. And if the viability of Christian marriage is questioned, then every other promise in the Word of God becomes suspect. Believers will then be unable to put their whole weight down on their faith.

It is for this simple reason that this book attempts to say to Christian people who are caught in troubled marriages: Let's try harder, because we need to reverse this terrible trend. Divorce not only causes a number of well-documented social ills, but is close to destroying the very basis of our Christian faith. What's at stake here is not simply the happiness of one or two people, but rather the very nature of *our* relationships, our *children's* relationships, and our *grandchildren's* relationships with God. I believe we owe each other a second, greater effort—another reasonable try toward the establishment of fidelity within the marriage bond and a stable foundation for our children and our families.

I also believe that if you are reading this Introduction, whether you have purchased this book or simply decided to examine its contents, the event has not happened by coincidence. In some mysterious way, the Holy Spirit has already begun to direct you toward a more healthy marriage. Though there may be great pain in your life—even ample reasons to "chuck it all" and give in to the readily available "solution" of divorce—maybe you have decided to think about it a little more deeply.

I hope you will be open-minded enough to consider giving your troubled marriage another chance. I believe God will honor your desire. This book is written with my prayer that as you read, you will identify salvageable areas within your own relationship that will cause you to put to work some of the resources available to the Christian. The rescue of even one couple from divorce would make all of the effort involved in this book worthwhile.

THE QUESTION BEHIND THE QUESTION

It is impossible to truly assess the consequences of "putting asunder what God has joined together." The common questions that people ask are, "Does the Bible permit divorce?" or "Does God allow for remarriage?" Often these questions are asked without regard for the consequences. They are important questions, of course, and are especially critical to the Christian within the framework of *obedience*. In this book, however, *we are trying to work with the question behind the question*.

Our main concern is not, "What can I get by with and still be allowed to enter heaven?" We should be more interested in asking, "Are my actions motivated by true commitment to Jesus Christ and concern for His kingdom, or are they selfishly aimed at finding answers at the expense of others?" Most of us, when asked about our actions directly, would say that we wish to be responsible about what we do. But the truth of the matter is that too few of us really care how our actions affect loved ones.

Very often in times of deep confusion, pain, selfishness, and anger, we do things that hurt others far more than we can imagine. In this book, I'll be asking you to honestly look at your actions and apply your will toward the healing and refinement of your marriage—before it reaches the disaster state.

One of my friends is a lawyer who handles mostly divorce cases. He is also a deeply committed Christian. Often he has told me, "My firm doesn't break up marriages; we simply bury dead ones." I suppose he is right. Yet over the years this lawyer has sent to me many couples whom he felt could save their marriage. Happily, we have had a rather impressive success record of bringing these people back to their original state with healed relationships and restored marriages.

If your marriage still has any life at all and if your present slide toward divorce has not come to the point of no return, then the application of truth and effort may well provide the basis you need. Your marriage may yet become what you so dearly intended it to be when you stood at the altar and made vows to God and to one another.

I know from experience that it is possible. We shall begin by discussing some foundational ideas to provide the basis for the restoration of your marriage to what you, your spouse, and God want it to be.

CHAPTER ONE

Don't Think 'Too Late' Too Soon

I'm convinced that most people could endure any level of pain, sadness, or disappointment if they thought that a day would come when the pain would be over. We all make bargains based on short-term discomfort—in the dentist's chair or during times of sickness, for example. We simply look toward the moment when the dentist will finish drilling, when the flu passes, or when the surgery is successfully completed. Then we can get on with life in a normal way. But when there seems to be no letup in our suffering and we can't foresee a solution, the pain sometimes grows unbearable. Hopelessness becomes debilitating.

REFLECTION AND REGRET

I remember sitting with a friend who had invited me to his country club for dinner. The Christmas season was approaching, and the club was decorated in a festive fashion. A large Christmas tree in the lobby was lavishly decorated. Tasteful bows and colorful holiday trimmings were everywhere. A simmering bowl of spicy cider was centered on a buffet table, adding a wonderful "Christmasy" smell to the dining room. Soft, orchestral music played familiar music in a sequence of carols. This place seemed to me like a very inviting place to have a beautiful Christmas dinner.

But I soon discovered that my friend didn't feel the same way. Despite the decorations, the aromas, the sounds, and the beautiful atmosphere, he told me that Christmas is one of the toughest times of year for him.

"Why is that?" I asked.

He replied, "Because I know I have to spend it alone in this place."

I attempted to ease the situation, "Well, I guess if you have to suffer, this is surely the place." I smiled and gestured toward the chef who stood near us. He wore a starched, tall, white hat and cut generous slabs of juicy, rare roast beef. Colorful, delicious samplings of numerous gourmet foods were laid out for our enjoyment.

As I looked around to see who else was dining, I saw the other country club members. Exciting people—the notable "movers and shakers" of the community—were our company. My friend was well-liked, even loved, by those who knew him. He should have been genuinely happy. Yet, here he was with chin on his chest, pouring out his concerns to me.

His unhappiness was not new, of course. I had heard the same thing before, dozens of times, from many others. I knew his story intimately, and I knew what to expect. Most pastors and people in the counseling professions hear these same stories during every holiday season. They hear incredible outpourings of sadness during these times.

My friend's story was typical of them all. He told me about his first marriage. "I guess we just drifted apart. My wife and I developed what our attorneys called 'irreconcilable differences.' I'd become wrapped up in my business. You know?"

I nodded and listened as he continued: "I guess I felt I was simply trying to do my duty, you know—earning a living, becoming successful, buying things we needed."

My friend looked off in the distance for a moment, reflecting. "It's funny," he said, "my family never turned down the things I bought. In fact, sometimes I felt like I was the only person in the family who really did care enough to provide for their way of life."

I thought of his family and knew what he meant. They had the country club membership, a couple of luxurious cars, and an elegant, spacious home with a swimming pool. The children had all the right labels on their clothing, and attended the right private schools. His wife bought her clothes in the best stores. He had even given her a few baubles that showed off their success—jewelry, a fur coat, and material things that are so desirable.

But as my friend commented wryly, "None of this made any real difference. I can't explain it, but our marriage—which began as an exciting and happy relationship—turned into dust before our very eyes. I even enjoyed going away on business trips because it had become easier for me to relate to other businessmen. So I began to find excuses to stay away from home more and work late."

He paused for a moment, cleared his throat, and continued. "My wife began to develop her life in the same way. Eventually, our marriage ended in divorce. It just sort of died quietly. After a few months, I remarried and so did she. I still saw her at various social events, concerts, school events—things the kids were involved in. I'd see her on that other man's arm and realize that he had taken *my* place with *my* family. Since she had custody of the kids, I could only see them on certain weekends and a few weeks during the summer."

He shook his head, "Somehow I can't seem to put together the kinds of activities that excite the kids. When we get together, things are awkward and sometimes pretty tense. My own children can make me feel like an outsider. Maybe it's fortunate that my new marriage has produced no children."

He picked at his meal and sighed. "I was able, even after child support and extra expenses, to get myself a better car. I have a sailboat at the marina. And my new wife is somewhat younger, so I enjoy the idea of 'showing her off' around town, you know? Things aren't all bad."

He paused for a moment. "But when I try to go to church and be with our former friends, I feel guilty, as if something is wrong between my friends and me. I know it's not my new wife's fault, but my second marriage just isn't providing the happiness that I hoped for."

My friend sat silently for several minutes, his eyes somewhat misty and with regret. Then he continued, "You know, Jay, I often see my former wife with this other guy. And even though I know we're divorced and she has every right to be with him, I really resent him. It looks to me like they're really happy. I get a horrible sinking feeling because I thought our divorce would solve a problem, but it didn't. I feel like I've lost it all. I'm convinced that if we had tried harder at our first marriage . . ." and his voice trailed off.

Then he said something that seemed extremely insightful. "You know, Jay, we should have tried harder." After a pause he added, "I think we tend to marry the right person the first time around. What do you think?"

I nodded, "Yes, I've noticed that people usually do have some kind of intuitive sense when they pick their mate. And spending time to make that relationship work is far superior to giving up."

He agreed. "I guess every marriage starts out with all of the anticipation and excitement of new love. But when things dry up or go sour, it somehow seems easier to throw it all away and start over."

He went on, desiring to have me understand his real feelings at this moment. "You know, Jay, on Christmas we're going to have Christmas dinner here at the club. My new wife is from another part of the country. She's not close to her family, so we don't visit them at Christmas. And rather than having my family with me, the kids will be with their mother."

His eyes revealed his true thoughts, which were locked on a memory of times past. "They'll be in the house with a Christmas tree. . .the smells of Christmas cookies and turkey. . .all the happiness. . .everything that makes Christmas special. And this year I'll be here in the midst of these decorations, drinking too much and secretly wishing that I could be there—in what I really feel is *my home*, with *my wife* and *my kids*."

He threw his napkin down decisively, "But it's all gone now. There's no way to get it back, is there?"

Sadly I had to agree. "No. I don't think there is. In fact, I think breaking up your new marriage trying to restore your first one might even be worse than the scenario you've just laid out to me."

Unfortunately, I've heard this man's story many times, with all kinds of variations. Stories like his give me the feeling that marriage is worth fighting for, even against our own better "inclinations," against our own will, against our own desires, against virtually anything. It is worth the fight to save a marriage—if only to keep ourselves from having to go through the sadness this man and so many others have described to me.

Years have gone by now, and my friend and I stay in touch. His children are grown and he is a grandfather. Yet I can't help but wonder how he really feels about it all, especially since he laid bare his true feelings to me on that one desperate day.

DON'T WAIT TO DEAL WITH YOUR PROBLEMS

What is it like to feel like the "third wheel"? To try and explain to grandchildren who this man is who doesn't live with Grandma? To see them wonder about this man who shows up, tries to hold them, tries to say things and do things and buy things and be with them? But this man doesn't fit on the family tree. He is a broken branch sitting at the edge of family life.

Is marriage worth fighting to keep? Yes! Absolutely! At all costs, put up a fight! From this moment on say, "I will not give in to my feelings, even though I have every legitimate reason to have these feelings. Though I actually deserve to be rid of the unhappiness that I feel at this moment in this relationship, I won't give up on this marriage."

Dr. Bernard Harnik makes the following observation in his very helpful book, *Risk and Chance in Marriage* (Word Books):

> Theoretically it may be true that divorce and remarriage will result in a more profound and maturing experience the

second time. I have seen very few instances of this in practice. Usually the divorced person will choose a similar partner the second time, will behave about the same, and make the same mistakes. Even when because of shame or the fear of developing a bad reputation, the second marriage does not end in divorce, the growth process is stopped. . . .The partners just give up in resignation. Such resignation in marriage is the expression of the blocking of the maturing process and results in further delay of any further maturation.

I would argue, from Dr. Harnik's observations as well as from my experience in dealing with hundreds of couples over the years, that now—during the *current marriage*—is the time to begin to deal with the maturation process. You ought not think that this process can be speeded up simply by changing marriage partners. *This* is the time to make a stand. *Now* is the time to start working for genuine solutions. Your present marriage is real and can be healed. Don't count on your problems being solved by some theoretical marriage to take place in the future.

If you and I were sitting face-to-face in my study right now, perhaps you'd say, "Jay, you just don't understand what kind of situation I'm in."

And I'd reply, for sake of argument,"Don't jump from the frying pan into the fire."

AN UNEXPECTED CHAIN REACTION
Marriage is a difficult task, but it may well be easier than other options. Let's look at what is involved once you take that first step toward divorce, having given up on the marriage you now have. Think about what a "blended" scenario means in your relationships.

In most cases, both you and your current spouse will remarry. The relationships have suddenly become more complicated. You have a new spouse. You also have a former spouse and your new spouse's former spouse. Now you must deal with two new people and two new relationships, because these people don't cease to exist. If you are married and have children, the situation becomes even more complicated. There may be children from *your* former marriage, and if your new spouse has had children, you must also consider *those* people.

Now we've added an entirely new dimension: children for whom you have responsibility, yet who are not necessarily your own. Perhaps these are youngsters with whom you have not developed any rapport. They may defy your authority or even resent you at every level.

Your children, because of custody and visitation laws, can visit your former spouse. The same anger, hurt, confusion, and rebellion often show up in such relationships. If your former spouse has married someone who has children, now your children must get to know and relate to those children by that former marriage. If you are young, you and your new spouse may have children. The same is true of your former spouse and the spouse's new mate.

So now the scenario becomes extremely complicated, including:

• The children you and your former spouse have already had

• The children your new spouse has already had

• Children you and your new spouse may have together

• Your former spouse's children from his or her new spouse's previous marriage.

• Your former spouse's new children with his or her new spouse.

If any of these adults have been married more than once before, the situation becomes more complicated, in geometric fashion. No wonder our newer generations are so confused and vulnerable.

I have spent hundreds of hours listening to people describe this scenario. I usually end our conversations by saying, "If you think you are going to solve the complex problems of your life by trading in your current relationship for a new one, stop kidding yourself. You haven't taken time to think through the kinds of headaches, heartaches, and nightmares that come to the most responsible of people when they choose divorce too quickly. Such a choice immediately places the person into the worst kind of complex, human drama. The results are almost universally catastrophic.

Lots of people affirm that once they get a divorce, they won't get married again. The memory of their recent pain is great. Yet it's virtually impossible for a previously married person to return to a single status. Certain needs and cravings cry out for the human intimacy the person has already experienced.

It is almost inevitable that a divorced person will eventually remarry. Often the person runs into someone very much like the former spouse—someone who meets the same basic needs that were met by the first marriage. Only now with a new person, common hurts and heartaches are shared. Since that person seems to understand the divorced person's pain, the tendency is usually to take another chance and enter into marriage again. But the initial problems that made the first marriage fail are still unsolved.

This repetition of failure sometimes occurs three and four times. I believe this is why God gave us the biblical admonition to avoid divorce. God is not a heavenly spoilsport, telling us not to do certain things just to keep us from having a good time. His instructions are to help us, not to hinder us.

When a couple opts for divorce, they open themselves to all kinds of pain, most of which have no solution at all. Divorce creates never-ending grief. The loss of a spouse through death is final. The period of grief after a loved one dies will end. But in divorce, the grief might never end so long as the two formerly married persons are alive. Sometimes it gets even worse.

Jim and Sally Conway recount a humorous situation in their excellent book, *Your Marriage Can Survive Mid-Life Crisis* (Thomas Nelson Publishers), quoting a newspaper article headlined, "Computer Sets Up Couple for Rematch." The article went on to say:

Maybe computers know best. A man who divorced his wife after a bitter six-year court battle and turned to a computer service to find himself the ideal mate was surprised when from two thousand prospective brides, the machine selected his former wife.

"I did not know that my ex-wife had been the ideal counterpart for our marriage. I decided to give it a try by being more tolerant toward her."

The couple's first marriage lasted twenty-one years, (but they were) divorced nine months ago due to severe disharmony after living apart for six years.

Each one, without the other knowing, turned to the same municipal computer matching service to find a new partner.

BACK TO BASICS

Rather than focusing your attention on what's wrong with your marriage, it might be better to ask some basic questions: Why did we get married in the first place? What did we see in each other? Why did we want to be together all the time? Why did we want to commit ourselves to a marriage relationship? Why did we want to share things and spend time with each other?

If you can dig through all the emotional debris and get back to the initial glow of your first love, you will always find something worthwhile. People simply don't proceed into marriage, in most cases, without having some solid reasons.

Later those solid reasons may become layered over because of anger, resentment, or hostility. But if you can identify these problems and begin to remove the layers, there's a good chance for some new beginnings that will enrich the relationship you now have. You can be saved from the kinds of heartaches that arise from a complicated remarriage.

One of the most commonly shared bits of wisdom I hear when I am talking to older married couples (30 to 50 years together) goes something like this: "We got married in the old-fashioned way. When we were wed, divorce

27

was not an option. Our families simply did not accept divorce. Neither did the church."

When people say these things, I'm reminded that often what we recall as "the good old days" is actually a result of our poor memory. Indeed, in those days were couples who got divorced, but they were simply forgotten about or ignored. In fact, at one time the church was so resistant to divorce that when couples in the community were divorced, they simply disappeared. The local family of God was unforgiving on this matter and divorced people were all but drummed out of the congregation.

This is unfortunate. I would much rather see the church dealing with the problems of divorce than see people estranged from the family of God. Yet there is wisdom in affirming that divorce should not be an option as we ask ourselves, "Is my marriage worth trying to save?"

Dr. James E. Kilgore, a well-known family counselor from Atlanta, Georgia, makes the following observation in his book, *Try Marriage Before Divorce* (Word Books):

> I am convinced that the majority of couples cannot be emotionally committed to each other because they have yet to settle the divorce issue. Few married people have not experienced the question of what being divorced is like. Some envy single people. Trying in marriage begins with that sense of commitment which says, "I do not have to live with you, but I choose to happily." That declaration of intent supported by a disciplined course of seeking mutual supportiveness brings full joy to a couple. The escape hatch for marriage has been locked down. Maybe it needs to be checked regularly, but it will not be opened in the trials under the sea of life's pressure. Its secure fasteners represent the continuing commitment of the couple to seek marital pleasure with each other. Often it is the subtle pleasure to please others rather than our partner that tempts us to use the escape hatch of divorce.

I believe Dr. Kilgore has hit on a basic issue. He reaffirms the wisdom observed by the many experienced couples who commit to the idea that divorce is not an option. When divorce is an option in our mind, we will always find ways to use it to walk away from our problems rather than seeing our way through them.

I've often said in churches where I speak that divorce in a family is like a virus. If one person "catches" it, then a sister, brother, children, or others will also be "infected."

People often justify divorce by saying, "My sister got a divorce and it didn't kill her. She survived and got out of a bad situation. Now I'm facing some of those same difficulties, so I'll use the same method." In the same way that you can picture the United States Department of Health putting pins in a map tracing a flu virus across the country, divorce will sweep through a church because someone said, "Divorce is okay."

Divorce sweeps through an entire culture the same way, as people try to follow the path of least resistance. My observation is that what seems to be the path of least resistance may actually have more difficulty and grief than if one had chosen to struggle with and work through the marriage problems in the first place.

COMMITMENT NOW PROVIDES HOPE LATER

I am pleading for the commitment on the part of each reader to struggle with marriage problems until a solution is found, to refuse even to consider divorce as a possible option. It's only with this sense of "there's no other way out" that we will see our way through for long-lasting marriages in our modern world.

We face too many bad role models and examples, too many temptations, too many well-meaning people encouraging us to give up. What better reason for us to "hang in there" than because we take seriously what we said before God and witnesses at the marriage altar? Would you be willing to say, "I plan to commit myself to this marriage—even if it involves pain, even if it involves inequities and unfairness. I will give this marriage every possible chance to succeed rather than immediately looking for a way out."

I'm not only attempting to remind you of the commitment you made at the marriage altar, but I'm also trying to appeal to your common sense and self-interest. It really is in your self-interest not to complicate your life with new relationships that are potentially more difficult and painful than the ones you are trying to resolve now.

Jim and Sally Conway again help us understand the slippery path toward the break-up of our marriages. Once more from their book, *Your Marriage Can Survive Mid-Life Crisis*, they observe:

> Marital collapse seems to follow predictable steps toward the ultimate destruction of the marriage. This is verified in a study of marital burnout which lists these stages:
>
> 1. Unrealistic expectations characterized by partners who hold high expectations of what the relationship should be and how the spouse should fulfill their needs.
>
> 2. Manipulation. Attempt to make the other spouse conform to his or her expectations. This phase is usually volatile and intense as each spouse continues to believe that each partner can and must be changed.
>
> 3. Hostility. Anger marked by detachment and a gnawing sense of futility.
>
> 4. Hopelessness. Resisting suggestions to improve. In despair they either experience emotional divorce, feel trapped while staying together, or conclude that actual divorce would be less painful.
>
> In more than thirty years of counseling experience, we have seen a consistent pattern of people not looking for help in the early stages of marital trouble, but waiting until things are desperate. If they seek help in the hostility stage, they come with much disillusionment, but still with a glimmer of hope. If they don't seek help

until the hopelessness stage, they usually are in total despair; in fact, they may be using the counselor as an authority figure to verify that their marriage is a failure and to justify getting a divorce.

Before reaching the stage that my lawyer friend calls "burying dead marriages," or simply looking for an escape hatch, or seeking from a counselor the "justification" for a way out of your marriage, let's look at how people get into this situation in the first place.

CHAPTER TWO

The Source of Our Pain

I once saw a lab experiment that has haunted me ever since. A science technician had electrified the bottom of a cage filled with white mice. By turning a switch, he could transmit a heavy electric shock to them.

The mice were, of course, oblivious to the threat. They wandered around the cage doing mouse-like things: sniffing, exploring, eating, and drinking. Then the scientist suddenly flipped the switch and I watched in amazement as the mice were instantly transformed. Their placid world was shaken violently.

At first they only looked bewildered and frightened. But soon they began *attacking* each other. They tore at each other's ears and tails, and pulled each other's hair. Stunned by the electric shock, the mice rolled around squealing and nipping at one another viciously.

When the technician turned off the electrical current, the mice shook themselves and became more subdued. But they avoided one another and looked at each other with suspicion. Eventually they went about their business again, but with a sense of distrust of the other mice.

The scientist flipped the switch again. The mice once more felt the electrical current. Again they resumed combat with the mice nearest them. In many ways, the experiment seemed quite cruel, yet the response of the mice made sense.

RECOGNIZE HARMFUL OUTSIDE INFLUENCES

A refrain played on countless jukeboxes the world over goes something like, "Why do I hurt the one I love?" I've decided that the reason we hurt others—many times the very people we love the most—is that there are outside forces "charging up our cage," as it were. We don't understand these outside forces, in the same sense the mice didn't understand what was happening to them. They had never taken a course in electricity nor seen a picture book with Ben Franklin flying a kite in a lightning storm. The mice only knew there was a strange, baffling, cruel force at work. We occasionally encounter forces that are just as baffling.

Often we find ourselves in combat with those nearest to us—our spouses and family members—because we have not taken the time to understand the forces that are at work in our lives. We should keep in mind that although understanding is only one part of the solution, it is an important part. We need to understand what is happening around us before we can act responsibly.

It is my premise that it is often outside "shocks" that disturb us greatly and cause pain—not something caused by our spouses. But unwittingly, we turn on those closest to us. We claw and scratch and tear at them, when in fact, our source of pain is really something in the bottom of our cage that we don't understand.

Let's take the situation of a married couple living together for fifty years, raising children and grandchildren until they celebrate their golden anniversary. Actually, the idea of being married for fifty years is relatively new. It is an ideal that has been reached by many of our parents' generation, but it was simply not achievable for many people historically. In 1600, for instance, the typical 60-year-old man married four wives before he died. He wasn't polygamous nor prone to divorce. Society was simply harder on women than it is today, and they died younger. So the man of 1600 probably had four ten-to-twelve-year marriages.

Through the advances in modern medicine, public health, hygiene, diet, and relative peace on earth, we are unlike our forebears. From a purely physical standpoint, we have all the right elements to live together for a longer time. Staying together is a major challenge, quite different from our great-great-great-great grandfathers who committed themselves to several different women for shorter periods of time.

I also believe that we have other problems that are significantly more difficult than those faced by people living in an earlier and simpler time in history. For example, look at our social and economic realities. To support the life-style most of us have chosen, both spouses usually have to work.

Over half of all mothers in our country work outside the home. The old cliché used to be, "Man works from dawn till setting sun, but woman's work is never done." That quaint description of housework wasn't intended to address the wife's work done for an employer, outside the home, where demands are identical to those on the husband. These days both husband and wife are trying to please bosses, and they face tremendous pressures.

And most men have no model of a male who helped with the housework and did the dishes. In spite of the many articles written to convince us to change our male-female stereotypes, many men in our society don't seem to be responding. Numerous marriages are troubled by pressures brought about by the fact that wives are working full-time jobs. Working women are tired at the end of the day—just like working men. Yet they are still expected to be homemakers and mothers way into the night. The men, on the other hand, may sit watching television expecting their wives to wait on them. After all, that's how they remember home life with their fathers and grandfathers before them.

These patterns are not easy to break. They are very real. They build resentment and put stress on couples and families. Often, by simply taking a look at the situation, these problems can be resolved. In fairness to both husband and wife, there should be balance between the number of hours each puts forth in a given week, both at the job outside the home as well as household duties.

I am impressed at how many younger men today observe this need and work toward equal divisions of labor within the modern family. Nonetheless, pressures may return even after we think we've dealt with them. We need to confront them every day, because of the serious way they affect our marriages and the way we live. Working outside the home in order to support a way of life should cause us to reevaluate the stresses that this puts on our marriages.

Some interesting facts from our culture seem to have bearing on this subject. Experts tell us there are more mental problems among unmarried men than among married men. But there are more married women seeking mental counseling than unmarried women. Do we take this to mean that marriage brings about mental problems for women, but seems to solve them in men's lives?

CAREER IDENTITY VS. RELATIONSHIPS

In addition to the stress problem, there is the related concern of career orientation. If you asked a man a generation ago, "Why do you go to work," he would probably answer, "To support my family."

Today if you stood in the back of most churches, you could ask men the same question and get an infinite variety of answers. Many of them now answer in relationship to their career. Their identity is based on what they do: "I'm a banker"; "I'm a teacher"; "I'm an engineer"; or "I'm a physician."

These men will tell you they are fulfilling their career expectations and have been programmed to be extremely loyal to their vocations (a product of the work of industrial psychologists and other counselors). It has even come to the point where many of us have lost our identity because it has been sublimated to our career orientation.

In a church where I was pastor for some years, we discussed this very issue. We discovered that each career seems to have various levels of hierarchy. People measure themselves and others by what rung of these various ladders they and others are positioned on.

Our town had an ice-cream store, and everyone remarked that the ice-cream store was the place where everyone was on common ground. Brain surgeons, carpet tackers, business executives, and housewives were all on the same level at the ice-cream store. There was no hierarchy.

As pastor I used this illustration one Sunday as a challenge, and added that the real common ground ought to be at the foot of the cross. The church ought to be the place where people can come, feel accepted, and be totally relaxed as to who they are. They should be able to participate without having to be evaluated, ranked, and put into some hierarchy of importance based on career.

So as an experiment in our church, we began to say, "There's no such thing as a *justa*." (This expression came from people saying, "I'm just a teacher," "I'm just a homemaker," "I'm just a farmer," "I'm justa . . . ." When our people accepted that there's no such thing as a "justa," we then insisted that in church we call each other by name. We made it "illegal" to use a title or position as identification. No one was allowed to say, "My name is Doctor So-and-So" or "I'm Vice President of Whatever Company." At first some people felt naked and unimportant—unable to communicate without their career orientation crutch. But in about six months, most of us were able to stop thinking of ourselves in terms related to our careers.

The same problem can affect two people involved in trying to make a marriage work. Usually the man feels—but in many cases both man and woman feel—the pressure to declare identity based on career orientation. As a result of this outside influence, it becomes difficult for each one to make the other seem special for who the person is rather than what he or she does. In God's eyes there is no such hierarchy. Housewife, salesclerk, corporation president, and hotel maid have equal status. But when we are conditioned to think one role is more significant than another, the marriage relationship between two working people becomes strained.

This seems to be a force larger than ourselves. It involves our entire society. It puts pressures on us that make it difficult for us to put our loyalties in line. Though our pastors exhort us to put God first, then spouse, then family, and finally career, I'm convinced that most of us find ourselves a pawn to this idea of career orientation.

MOBILITY

In today's world, industry demands mobility. In families where the father is under forty years of age, the family tends to move about every three years. Our culture, therefore, doesn't have deep roots, and people may respond with feelings of insecurity and low self-esteem. In fact, experts tell us that mobility can even affect communication between man and wife. Their understanding of each other's needs and desires can be severely hampered by pressures brought about by career mobility.

The wife often feels she is a victim of someone else's decision. A faceless, mysterious entity in a strange city far away is telling her to do something she fears and resents. She feels she is being forced to tear up her roots and move, regardless of how *she* feels.

The wife is also often asked to give up her own job so her husband can make a career move. But she is also career oriented and her work means a great deal to her. All in all, a family move can unleash terrible anxiety and bad feelings. The wife especially finds this pressure intense.

Suppose a youngster buys his mother a geranium on Mother's Day. She plants it in the front yard, but the next day she grows tired of it being in the front yard, so she digs it up and moves it to the side yard. A day or two later Mom moves the geranium to the other side yard. By the end of the week, she moves it to the backyard. If Mom moves that geranium enough, it goes into shock, and the shock of each move becomes deeper than the previous one. Eventually the geranium just gives up and dies. A gardener might point out that all the little rootlets have been broken off. Each time the flower is moved, more roots are damaged, making it impossible for the plant to take nourishment. Without food it simply cannot grow, and it eventually dies.

Human beings operate much the same way. If a wife has been moved from city to city—a while here, a few years there—very often she loses her ability to put out roots. She senses a series of shocks that can be deadly to her marriage and emotional health.

NEGLECT

I remember having a woman come to me and say of her husband, "He has destroyed me."

I asked, "What do you mean?"

She replied sadly, "Everything I do is unimportant. I try to tell him about the broken screen door, a leaky faucet, or the garage door opener that won't work. He just says, 'Call the man. I'm too busy.' He doesn't seem to understand that everything I do is this kind of stuff. I spend my whole life on things that he thinks are trivial because, after all, he is doing important things. His time and energy belong to his job. And as a result, he makes me feel unimportant. He has destroyed me."

The woman looked down at the floor and tears welled up in her eyes. "Everything I used to be as a person has been killed. My whole life is gone because of his neglect."

I am convinced that her husband surely didn't intend to cause his wife to feel hopeless. Yet his inattention resulted in her despair.

DOMINATION

This male-female identity struggle occurred with the wife who worked in the home. Other men feel emasculated by the fact that their wife is helping to support the family. At a primal level, men seem to feel that they are unable to pull their weight like their fathers or grandfathers had done. Especially in traditional, multigenerational blue-collar families, men tend to think (even if they don't express) that, "Woman's place is in the home." They even confuse this assumption for biblical values and interpret the tradition as a means of being dominant over their wives. But Jesus never gave husbands *unconditional* authority over their wives.

You might see examples of male domineering in public. Sometimes a man attacks his wife verbally. Other times he finishes her sentences or puts her down when she tries to express herself. It's as though he has to say, "I want to bring you down a peg or two because, after all, I'm the man in this family. I am the important person, and I can't have someone else taking a leadership role for me." At a rational level, most husbands would find this way of thinking to be exceptionally cruel and unthinkable, but most do it without realizing it.

When a woman gives in to such mandates by quitting her job and coming home, she often loses something of herself in the process. The husband has taken away her self-worth. After all, she spent years getting a college degree or learning to perform a unique skill which society promised would give meaning to her life. Suddenly she finds herself "just a housewife," one of those "barefoot and pregnant" people who is constantly harassed and made fun of by the media.

It's no wonder she feels tremendous tensions in her marriage. If she loves the career for which she was prepared and which makes her feel like a person of value, what hope does she now have? Severe depression will almost always follow when a person is in a hopeless situation.

THE MEDIA MODEL

The media affects our perceptions in this regard. If you follow the TV soaps, you realize that day after day the same scenarios are played out—housewives are home taking care of the babies while their husbands are lunching with beautiful, poetic, highly educated, articulate, sophisticated women. Suddenly, through all of this intimacy in the workplace, the husband develops a relationship with a new woman—one who is sympathetic that he is stuck with a woman at home who simply has not grown along with him.

It doesn't take long before the scenarios on TV take effect. Housewives identify with the significant pain of these situations, and often become easy prey for those who would traffic on their vulnerability and lead them into illicit affairs. After all, why should they live hopeless, quiet, futile lives while their husbands become more and more sophisticated? When men feel they have outgrown their wives and women feel left behind, the result is an agonizing tension within the marriage.

The media is also responsible for a very distorted view of love today. They suggest that "love is a feeling." They tell us that "happiness is something you deserve." They continually affirm that "duty is secondary to your personal pleasure." As a result, we begin to think there must be something wrong with our marriage relationships unless they are constantly filled with one erotic experience after another.

We begin to feel emotions that are very real. To return to this chapter's opening illustration, the shock from the floor of our electrified cage is coming up through our feet, through our legs, and into our bodies. We don't understand it, but we feel something. So we respond by lashing out.

THE WRONG RESPONSE TO FAILURE

Sometimes people say they have a troubled marriage, when in fact, that's not the problem at all. It's just that they are together in a cage being manipulated by external forces. They are unable to determine their own destinies due to their very complicated situation.

Married couples face hundreds—if not thousands—of different pressures. It may easily be possible that they choose the wrong "enemy" at which to lash out. It is a tragedy to blame one's spouse, family, or friends for the pain they are experiencing. This is not to say that their pain is not real. In fact, their feelings of impotence and insecurity are often so real that they are driven to desperate acts.

I have listened to the stories of many dozens of men and women caught in marital triangles. In most cases it's the man who has been unfaithful to his wife. Often he has come seeking someone to help him find a way out of the trap he is in. A recent example reflects hundreds of previous cases.

The man began, "Jay, thanks for meeting with me. I hope you can help me."

"I'll try. What's the problem?"

"I . . . I'm having an affair."

"Go on," I encouraged.

The man seemed older than his 40 years. He looked down and avoided looking at me directly. "I know it's wrong," he admitted, seeming to grope for the right words to say. Then he smiled sheepishly. "It seems so blunt to admit to it. But the affair is only part of my problem."

For several moments he said nothing. When he saw that I was still listening, he began to talk some more. "I guess my real problem is impotence. . . ."

I interrupted, "That sounds like something your physician should. . . ."

He waved his hand and shook his head, clarifying himself. "I don't mean sexual impotence," he said. "Let's face it, everything I've tried to do has failed. *I'm* a failure. That's what I mean when I say I'm impotent."

I nodded my understanding and the man continued. "I've long since given up my childhood dream of becoming president of the United States," he grinned. "I've lost hope of becoming president of my company. Or even department manager. I've hit the wall."

"But you're doing all right, aren't you?" I offered.

He shrugged, "I don't know. The money's okay. . .and I can keep up with the pace. But. . . ." He looked away wistfully.

I asked him about his wife. "Have you talked with Donna about your feelings?"

He looked startled. I could tell he hadn't discussed his problems with her. After a pause he spoke quietly. "I guess I feel embarrassed to share this with Donna. In fact, it was easier for me to find another woman—someone who expects less than Donna. I tell her my problems, she listens, and I imagine that somehow this woman has compassion and empathy. That's how our affair began. She listened, and this empathetic relationship developed the appearance of real love. It wasn't long until we were involved sexually."

I almost laughed as he seemed to read my thoughts about that other woman. "You know, she's not at all good looking compared to Donna. We have absolutely nothing in common. We don't have the same compatibilities that Donna and I have. But here I am, deeply involved in a sexual affair."

I pointed out to him what seemed obvious to me. "You're involved in this sexual affair because Donna is tied to your career and your career has been thwarted. You feel a sense of impotence that needs a release, so you look to somebody else. You're trying to fulfill a need so deep and confusing that you don't even truly understand it. Your affair has nothing to do with love. It has nothing to do with sexuality. It has to do with the fact that you're caught in the midst of something more complicated. You've become a victim rather than an actor in your real life."

This man and I talked for a long while about his problems and feelings. Eventually he could see an outline for getting his life straightened out. But what could he have done before he became caught in this kind of dilemma? Not everyone who has feelings of impotence or frustration enters into a sexual affair. There must be other ways of expressing a deep sense of loss and failure.

LIVING WITH INTENTIONALITY

For the secular person, I am not sure there is a good answer. If success is the ultimate goal, people can try harder to be more competent in their professions and attempt to be more cunning, more focused. In doing so, they may be willing to cut out all the extraneous things from their lives. In fact, recently I was reading in a prestigious business journal that a man simply cannot be the president of a large company and have his life "cluttered" with a wife and family. According to the conclusion of the article, corporate leadership requires a man's full attention and involvement. This author said that perhaps we need to find a new generation of managers for major companies who are willing to give their whole lives to these values.

For the Christian, however, these conclusions are not acceptable. Over and over the Bible reminds us that true success is in what we are, not in our titles or possessions. I'm convinced that if we are going to find lasting solutions, we need a revolutionary readjustment of our entire value structure. We must reexamine what it means to be a Christian in our modern world.

A word I use a great deal these days is *intentionality*. I believe if we live purposeless, "willy-nilly" lives, we will be like water coming down a mountain seeking the path of least resistance. All the barriers put in our path will compromise and capture us. Without purpose or direction, we are easily channeled into a worldly life-style.

A Christian must have the courage of conviction to stop, examine his life and actions, and acknowledge that the Bible is not an archaic book. It is God's Word, not a mere collection of religious platitudes. It reminds us that we are strangers and pilgrims in a wicked and perverse generation. This shouldn't prompt us to cry "Woe is me," be belligerent about everything we do, or go around with some sort of religious chip on our shoulders. It does mean, however, that we should take a sober look at realities.

A FEW HARD QUESTIONS

First of all, how do you measure success? What are your real values? Are they eternal or material? Are people in your life more important than things? Is it important to keep up with the Joneses? Should you and your family seek a simpler, less materialistic life-style? Do you think your children need to be taught to live more frugally and not be caught in the trap of "bigger and better"?

Dr. Anthony Campolo speaks pointedly to these issues. The following quotation is taken from his book *The Success Fantasy* (Victor):

Because the world sees wealth, power, and prestige as the indicators of success, we have been conditioned to seek them with all of our might. But our Lord has different criteria for evaluating success. He calls us away from society's symbols of success and urges us to seek after "His kingdom and His righteousness" (Matt. 6:33). Many who are considered least important by society may find themselves sitting in places of honor at the great banquet feast in the world to come.

Wealth, power, and prestige can corrupt those who possess them. *Wealth* can delude us into a kind of self-sufficiency and denial of our need of God. It is easy to become so overly protective of our economic interests that we oppose compassionate social policies which would diminish our wealth.

Power can turn us into megalomaniacs. Desire to dominate others can lead us to diminish their humanity, as well as our own. Sometimes we sacrifice those who are nearest to us in order to achieve power.

Cravings for *prestige* can lead us into destructive pride and egotism that know no bounds, until our need for the world to focus on us becomes obnoxious.

Yet we must remember that wealth, power, and prestige have great potential for good. It is only their wrong use which is evil.

Though Dr. Campolo is speaking about Christian people in the social context of economic and political responsibility, these truths are all the more true within the family structure. Many marriages cannot be saved unless a couple is willing to allow Jesus Christ to radically transform their value system and life-style structure.

I have stated that this book is for Christians. Yet a person's Christianity must go beyond the desire to escape hell and go to heaven. A genuine conversion to Jesus Christ is one in which we give Him our trust. We become willing to say, "Dear Lord, I give myself to You in such a way that I will put my faith and confidence in Your values. And as I seek the values of the kingdom of God, I will trust You to provide the rewards and happiness for me so I can live a life that would be pleasing in Your sight."

Your prayer might even have a confession: "Lord, I have put my values into the wrong things and I have been seduced by the world's way of thinking. As a result, I am losing my life, my family, my happiness and my marriage as a result. But now I desire, God, to be Your disciple and escape these temptations."

It is only in the midst of this kind of a radical commitment to Jesus Christ that certain life habits, well-established worldly values, and wrongful behavior patterns can be broken. Again we ask the question, "Is marriage worth fighting for?" The answer is obvious. Yes, it is.

Then we ask another question. "What is really causing all of your pain? What are some of those forces 'outside your cage' that affect your marriage?" If your pain is derived from a non-Christian value system that is driving your life, then your Christianity and faith need to go beyond the salvation of your soul—they need to influence the very values to which you cling with such tenacity.

First Steps Toward a Solution

Every aspect of your life and being needs to be born again. To the non-Christian, this idea seems impossible. When Jesus first presented this concept, the intellectual seeker, Nicodemus, exclaimed, "Surely [a man] cannot enter a second time into his mother's womb to be born!" (John 3:4) As much as Nicodemus may have wanted a new and better life, the offer to be born again seemed preposterous—and too good to be true. Perhaps you have the same kinds of feelings about restoring a freshness in your marriage. Can your marriage be "born again"?

To once again quote Tony Campolo's book, *The Success Fantasy*, here is a beautiful explanation of the power of God in this context:

For several years I taught at an Ivy League university. One of my graduate students inadvertently spoke a truth which he himself did not comprehend. "Doctor, there is no way to undo damage done by faulty social conditioning in the early stages of childhood. The hurt created by parents can never be overcome. The only hope would be if the individual would be able to go back and start over again. If somehow the individual could be born again."

I responded by saying, "But that's the good news. Each of us can be born again." The Holy Spirit working in our lives can enable us to overcome what has been and to become what was otherwise impossible. Basic attitudinal structures can miraculously be broken down and new ones constructed. Deeply established negative images of the nature of God can be erased and new ones drawn in their place. The Scriptures teach that, "If any man is in Christ he is a new creature; the old things passed away; behold, new things have come!" (II Cor. 5:17)

I cannot explain the ways in which this miracle occurs. I cannot describe the work of the Holy Spirit. But I can tell you that I have seen the impossible happen. I have seen personality structures altered and new orientations and attitudes before God come into being.

I cannot explain the process, but I can point to the change that takes place when a person asks the resurrected Jesus, whom Christians claim is everpresent, to take possession of him, to invade his personality, to enter his psyche. Some of my fellow social scientists chide my convictions on these matters, calling them expressions of mysticism. It may be true that I am somewhat mystical; but to the scientifically minded, I can say that the results of surrendering to Jesus are empirically verifiable.

It is precisely this kind of radical conversion of social, economic, occupational, and vocational value structure that I appeal for. Are you willing to commit yourself to being "born again" in each of these areas, that Christ might use His power to save your marriage?

As I watched those mice in the scientist's electrified cage, I wished I could make the experience easier for them by explaining what was actually happening. I wanted to somehow give them a basic course in electricity. Maybe if they understood what was causing them so much pain, they would quit biting each other and apologize for what they had done. Maybe they would work together and try to unhook the electrical wires so this would not happen to them again.

Of course, these thoughts are pure fantasy. Mice are incapable of becoming electricians. But I don't give up as easily on human beings! We are the creations of a Holy God. In fact, the Bible says we are His crowning creation. So my appeal to anyone reading this book is to sit with your spouse and soberly discuss some of the issues mentioned in this chapter.

Perhaps it is time to ask forgiveness for blame we may have assigned for some of the pain and tension of daily living—for lashing out when unknown or uncontrolled forces electrify our cages. Maybe if husband and wife can learn to look beyond their own feelings and to the source of this anguish, they can begin the task of "unhooking the wires." They can choose to commit to a value system and life-style that are more Christian in orientation. I know this would relieve some of the pressures that have brought them to the point of anger, pain, frustration, or dissatisfaction—to the point where some are even considering divorce as perhaps their only remaining option. Maybe it's necessary to repent of a false value structure and confess to being caught in a complicated social or moral problem. Many will need to turn their backs on the "American tradition" of keeping up with the Joneses.

But in light of what is at stake in saving our marriages, we must do precisely these things. I can envision a couple sitting in their family room holding hands while reading these words, or lying in each other's arms in bed thinking about these things. I can almost hear them saying, "Let's take a look at our lives; let's back off, slow down, and reexamine our values. Let's reconstruct our relationship in such a way that we have a say in what we are after, rather than letting ourselves become victims of cultural forces and stresses that we don't truly understand. We already know that these have led us nowhere except to disillusionment in what we love the very most—the marriage that God has given the two of us."

Only after a couple has identified the source of their pain can they begin—together—to "unhook the wires" that cause their distress.

CHAPTER THREE

Feelings Follow Actions

I suppose all authors are fascinated with book titles. The first time I heard the title, *Happiness Is a Choice*, I was immediately intrigued. I went out and bought a copy of this fine book written by two qualified Christian professionals—Dr. Frank B. Minirth and Dr. Paul D. Meier.

I soon discovered there was more to the book than just a catchy title. It turned out to be most helpful—not just a listing of simplistic platitudes or pat answers. *Happiness Is a Choice* (Baker Book House) deals with the topic of depression. In fact, I think it's one of the finest books available for people suffering from depression. One section from the book provides a good beginning for this chapter:

> You don't do what you do because you feel the way you feel—you feel the way you feel because you do what you do. Think about that for a moment. In other words, your actions (godly actions or ungodly actions) will determine how you feel. If you choose to love your mate, for example, and choose to act lovingly and respectfully toward your mate, the feeling of love will follow whether it was there before or not.
>
> Therapists have often tended to go to one extreme or the other in dealing with people's feelings versus their behavior. Some therapists (such as psychoanalysts)

emphasize feelings, whereas others (such as therapists from the schools of behavior modification or reality therapy) emphasize behavior. We believe both should be dealt with.

I could not agree more. In fact, this distinction is one of the reasons that the Bible is such a powerful book in my life. It is also why I say that there is hope for Christian marriages that is not available to non-Christian people. The Bible deals realistically with this connection between feelings and actions. God's Word continually commands us to love one another. In the Bible, love is not something you *feel*; love is something you *do*.

THE MANDATE TO LOVE

When you think about it, God would not command you to feel a certain way. Feelings are reactive; they occur as a result of something that happens to us. But love is active, so God can instruct us to perform that action and love others.

If you and your spouse were married in a church, it's very likely that sometime during the marriage ceremony, I Corinthians 13 was read. That great passage describes the attributes of love in terms of relationships, attitudes, and actions towards other people:

Love is very patient and kind, never jealous or envious, never boastful or proud, never haughty or selfish or rude. Love does not demand its own way. It is not irritable or touchy. It does not hold grudges and will hardly even notice when others do it wrong. It is never glad about injustice, but rejoices whenever truth wins out. If you love someone you will be loyal to him no matter what the cost. You will always believe in him, always expect the best of him, and always stand your ground in defending him (I Cor. 13:4-7, *The Living Bible*).

The expected behavior of the Christian is defined in the Bible by the word *love*. Jesus' words are recorded by

John: "And so I am giving a new commandment to you now—love each other just as much as I love you. Your strong love for each other will prove to the world that you are My disciples" (John 13:34, 35, *The Living Bible*). When we relate to one another in love, people will be amazed by the radical nature of our behavior.

For the sake of saving a marriage, it is absolutely imperative that we understand this point—that the love we are to show others, in obedience to Christ, is to be the same love that He has shown us. The foremost characteristic of God's love is that it is unconditional. This kind of love is so special that God even gave it a new name—grace.

If you've had any contact with a church, you can probably recite the standard definition: "Grace is the unmerited favor of God toward man." Man can do nothing to deserve God's love, yet God loves us just as we are. When we accept His love, He begins to transform us into His image:

> Let Christ Jesus be your example as to what your attitude should be. For He, who had always been God by nature, did not cling to His prerogatives as God's equal, but stripped Himself of all privilege by consenting to be a slave by nature and being born as mortal man. And, having become man, He humbled Himself by living a life of utter obedience, even to the extent of dying, and the death He died was the death of a common criminal. That is why God has now lifted Him so high (Philippians 2:5, *Phillips*).

LOVE NOT BASED ON PERFORMANCE

If we are to learn the lessons of love (and see our marriages saved by the power of Christ), we must understand the nature of Christian behavior and the power of Christ's love. The love of Jesus that we are supposed to imitate in our relationships is a love that is not only unconditional, but also one that empties itself of its own privileges and "prerogatives." This love humbles itself and becomes obedient to God.

This model of love is diametrically opposite to the self-seeking kind so prevalent today. Jesus said that people will know you are His disciples because this love is so radical (John 13:35). No one offers unconditional love to someone else on their own strength. Human love always has strings attached. In fact, most of us are conditioned to understand "performance love."

We are told, "I will love you more if you are a good boy than if you are a bad boy."

"I'll love you more if you get good grades than if you get bad grades."

"I'll love you more if you bring honor to this family than if you bring us dishonor."

"I will love you more as my husband if you talk to me than if you clam up."

But God's love never depends on our performance. His is the only kind of love that can radically transform your marriage and make it absolutely new.

Jesus Himself stirred up great controversy with His ideas almost 2,000 years ago. He told the Pharisees, "You have heard of old that it was said," and then He gave them a new concept, "But I say unto you. . . ."

Jesus said we are to turn the other cheek when attacked. If a man asks for our coat, we should also give him the shirt off our back. We are urged to walk the second mile, to give away what we have. Jesus said we are to love our enemies and do good to those who despitefully use us.

CONFLICTING ADVICE

These ideas were so radical in Jesus' day that His culture rejected them. They are just as repulsive to the non-Christian mind and culture of today. We have been told, "Nice guys don't win pennants," and that, "If you do good, people will take advantage of you."

Society's view of "love" is more calculating and self-serving. As a result, we study Jesus' words in Sunday school and church, but refuse to follow them in our marriages. Somehow we believe that if we take Jesus' advice, others will walk all over us.

We must learn to return good for evil and to love others in the way that Christ loved us. His love took Him to the cross, but He still loved us. Only when we surrender personal "rights" do we see how Jesus Christ can heal a marriage. And it begins when we in obedience treat others with love—regardless of how they treat us.

This is truly a radical challenge! But a dying or broken marriage needs a radical solution. Genuinely troubled marriages need more than the usual glib, pat clichés. People need a real, workable cure.

Lasting solutions to difficult problems are rarely easy. A ruptured appendix is a life-threatening crisis. A skilled surgeon can take care of the problem, but not without a sharp scalpel, a decisive removal of the source of the problem, and a reasonable period of recovery for the patient. Deadly cancer can sometimes be treated with chemotherapy, but usually not without severe side effects. On a physical level, there isn't always an easy way to deal with disease. In the same way, the treatment for troubled marriages is severe. Nevertheless, we must learn to apply the radical love of Jesus Christ to our lives.

This kind of love contradicts a great deal of modern psychological advice. We are told to, "Get in touch with your feelings. Be honest. Act in harmony with how you feel." A popular movement these days says a human being has "a right" to express his or her feelings in any situation. If you *don't* express your feelings, these psychologists tell us that then somehow you repress them and someday these sublimated feelings will come out in some harmful way later in your life.

The statements of Jesus Christ don't lose their impact in light of such modern psychological advice. The Bible makes more sense in regard to this discussion of feelings, actions, and responsible behavior. We are told precisely how we can get this concept working *for* us in a marriage, rather than *against* us.

PSYCHOLOGICAL MODEL: THE BEHAVIOR/FEELINGS CYCLE

The modern psychological model of feelings/behavior goes something like this:

1. You behave toward me in a certain manner, but I can't control your behavior. In fact, I am actually helpless when you act for or against me.

2. Your behavior produces certain feelings in me.

3. If I am in touch with my feelings, then I respond back toward you in relationship to these feelings. So if you do bad things to me, I feel badly and my behavior toward you may be filled with resentment, anger, or hostility. I respond to you based on my feelings.

4. Then, because I show you behavior that is full of hostility and anger, that behavior produces similar feelings in you.

5. So you then behave in turn toward me with behavior that is filled with more of the same anger and resentment. And we are caught in a descending spiral of hostility, even hate, toward each other because we chose to be "in touch with our feelings."

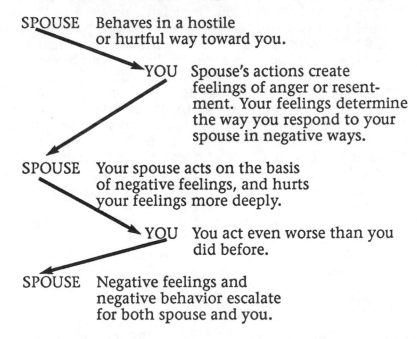

SPOUSE   Behaves in a hostile
         or hurtful way toward you.

YOU   Spouse's actions create
      feelings of anger or resent-
      ment. Your feelings determine
      the way you respond to your
      spouse in negative ways.

SPOUSE   Your spouse acts on the basis
         of negative feelings, and hurts
         your feelings more deeply.

YOU   You act even worse than you
      did before.

SPOUSE   Negative feelings and
         negative behavior escalate
         for both spouse and you.

BEHAVIOR ➝ FEELINGS ➝ BEHAVIOR ➝ FEELINGS

If we only follow the advice to "get in touch with our feelings," we may never learn to correct ourselves. Instead, we will find ourselves trapped by these ever-eroding, human relationships.

CHRISTIAN MODEL: THE BEHAVIOR/FEELINGS CYCLE

But the Christian model for resolving marriage conflict has another step, and it is essential that we understand it. The apostle Paul said: "In your anger do not sin: Do not let the sun go down while you are still angry" (Ephesians 4:26). Note that God does not command Christians to avoid anger. Becoming angry is a *reaction*, not an action. Anger is a feeling; love is an action.

If someone behaves toward me in an ugly or hostile manner, the action naturally produces feelings that are less than desirable. It is very natural for me to get angry. And while my feelings of anger are not improper, I must control them before I commit some kind of sin. As a Christian, I have the responsibility to add an obedience factor into the previous model.

In the modern psychological model, the sequence is simple—your behavior, my feelings, my behavior, your feelings. But in the Christian model we have a slight distinction—your behavior, my feelings, my behavior (which must always be checked by my obedience to act in a way that shows love), then your feelings.

So even if you act toward me in a destructive or sinful manner, I am instructed as a Christian to get my anger under control before I respond to you. I am to obey God and demonstrate love toward you, even if you do something hostile, hurt my feelings deeply, or make me feel resentment and deep anger.

The worldly psychological model, with its descending spiral of the ever-eroding feelings/behavior pattern is confused by the Christian model where angry feelings are controlled and the response is directed by love.

On the next page is a Christian model of the behavior/feelings cycle with the all-important extra step that changes the ultimate result.

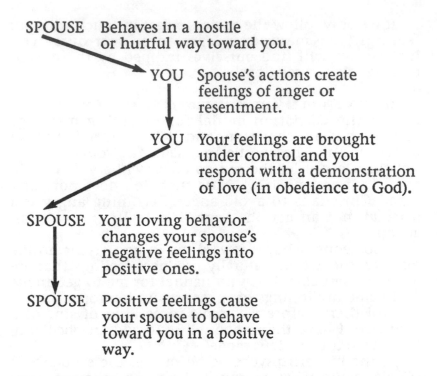

SPOUSE Behaves in a hostile or hurtful way toward you.

YOU Spouse's actions create feelings of anger or resentment.

YOU Your feelings are brought under control and you respond with a demonstration of love (in obedience to God).

SPOUSE Your loving behavior changes your spouse's negative feelings into positive ones.

SPOUSE Positive feelings cause your spouse to behave toward you in a positive way.

Most battles to save a marriage are lost in the interval between the time one of the spouses feels a certain way and responds based on those feelings. If he or she doesn't destroy the cycle by adding this extra step of obedience to God in the form of love, then the person is acting in a decidedly non-Christian manner. If there is no difference between Christians and non-Christians in the handling of conflict, how can we expect Christian marriages to do any better than secular ones?

Remember the biblical definition of love from I Corinthians 13: love is patient and kind, not jealous, doesn't brag, and isn't arrogant. Love doesn't act unbecomingly, doesn't seek its own way, and is not easily provoked. Our responses to our spouses must take on these characteristics if we are to overcome the feelings/behavior cycles that we experience every day of our marriages.

Norman Wright provides some practical ways of escaping this pattern in his book, *Seasons of a Marriage* (Regal):

It is not unusual for couples to develop such vicious circles. The result is that the harder each tries to deal with a problem, the worse it gets. Each person is emphasizing his own needs rather than the results of his actions. The more the wife nags and reminds her husband that the house needs painting or the garage needs cleaning, the more he seems to procrastinate. It is possible for a couple to break this negative behavior pattern if each is willing to submit to a very definite and specific program of action. Each spouse must identify his responsibility for his half of the problem. It will take time and work, but if what you are now doing is not working, then you have absolutely nothing to lose. The way to break the pattern is for each person to describe how the mate's behavior makes him or her react. When the two explanations are put together, each person may tend to become defensive. No one wants to hear that his own behavior is making his spouse behave in a negative manner. Therefore, it is important for each one to do his own analysis of the situation separately.

Here's a procedure which Dr. Carlfred Broderick of the University of Southern California suggests:

1. By yourself and in writing identify a problem between you and your spouse which meets the previous criteria of a vicious circle; that is, the harder you try to deal with the problem, the worse it gets.

2. From your point of view, describe what your spouse does or does not do that makes the problem worse.

3. Now write out in detail what it is that you do or fail to do either in response to what your spouse does or as an effort to change him.

4. You probably have some expectation as to what your spouse's response ought to

be to what you do in number three. What had you hoped that he or she would do?

5. What has been your spouse's actual response to your action or words?

6. What are your feelings about that response?

7. What keeps you from trying something new? What do you fear would happen if you tried something new? If you are on the receiving end of a request, why do you resist and howl? What would happen if you responded favorably to the request? Is the request really the problem, or is a power struggle occurring? How do you resist? Many people use what is called "passive-aggressive behavior." These include forgetting, withdrawing, neglecting, ignoring, or withholding. These are just as effective as a direct, outward, angry, or critical remark.

8. Write down at least two or three new responses that you could make. List a possible positive response on the part of your spouse to your positive change. It will be easy to think of a negative response like, "She'll never change," but this only wastes energy and cripples progress. List only positive responses. If you will act as if your partner is going to change in response to your positive change, there is a greater likelihood that the vicious circle will be eliminated.

It is important for a couple to see how they set up the vicious circle. Each person's behavior and the consequences of that behavior need full and careful exploration. As each person begins to see what his behavior is triggering in his partner and what a different response may do, then the cycle can be broken. In many cases changing the way we act even without full insight into the problem can lead to the discovery of a better way of relating. Part of the process of marital growth is to discover more effective ways of responding to each other.

This response to the vicious circle may seem difficult, but that's what it takes to replace irresponsible behavior with responsible behavior. You must discipline yourself to do this before love can begin to win out in any situation.

A story is told about a pastor who was being criticized by someone for certain parts of his ministry. In response he quoted this little poem:

He drew a circle that shut me out
Rebel, heretic, thing to flout
But love and I had a wit to win
We drew a circle that took him in
(Edwin Markham, 1852-1940).

This is the kind of spirit that will hold a marriage together. We need to be serious in our relationships, searching for answers to the truly terrifying problem of the breakup of our marriages. We need to take a closer look at the biblical instruction to obey Jesus Christ. It is through obedience we discover His simple formula—returning good for evil.

Keep in mind that we are in a real battle. Satan is our enemy. His goal is to disrupt lives, destroy marriages, and increase resentment between husbands and wives. By trying to break up our marriages, the devil opposes Christians, the church, and the transforming power of Jesus Christ to change lives and win people for eternity.

Professor David Augsburger has written a very useful book entitled *Caring Enough to Confront* (Regal). In his book he lists five approaches people use when they are involved in conflict:

(1) "I'm right and you're wrong." We all understand that one. We also know that it seldom leads to real solutions.

(2) "You win; I quit." We've all seen this attitude in relationships as well. Instead of continuing to address the problem, one of the partners gives in—but usually not without deep resentment and creating a "guilt trip" for the other person.

(3) The "doormat" or "peace at all costs" approach. One person always gives in to the other person, so conflict is never brought into the open. The stronger

personality always prevails and the truth never comes to light.

(4) "I'll meet you halfway." Surely this method is better than the previous three. But what if one person is entirely right and the other is all wrong? If they compromise halfway, they still don't reach the truth.

(5) "Caring enough to confront." This is Dr. Augsburger's suggested alternative. His whole book deals constructively with this matter of conflict. I encourage every family to have a copy of this useful book because it helps us with the very process we are discussing.

If there is one statement that sums up what I've been trying to say in this chapter, it is this: *For the Christian, behavior should not be a reaction to feelings, but rather obedience to the will of God.* I am always amazed when I hear people talk about committing their lives to Jesus Christ as their personal Savior when it is obvious that they don't apply any of His teachings to daily living. Yes, they accept His death on the cross to be the salvation for their sin. Yet it's as if they say, "Jesus, go ahead and die for me, but as far as the rest of my life is concerned, I'll live it myself."

The premise of this book is that Jesus Christ can heal our most troubling relationships if we are willing to obey Him. Our marriages can survive, but only if we truly understand and take action. If we refuse, we open ourselves to the secular forces that destroy lives everywhere. We open ourselves to the possibility of divorce, that awful trend that is creating the troubling statistics of separation that have become typical even of the Christian family.

It is possible that your marriage has caused you to suffer feelings of deep hurt, anger, neglect, or rejection. You may be the victim of betrayal and marital infidelity. You may feel alone or abandoned because your spouse is more interested in work, house, garden, children, friends, or relatives than in you. It may be that your needs are not being met.

I don't question the fact that your feelings are real. You may even have good reasons to feel as you do—

playing second fiddle to a business or another person. What I question is the wisdom of allowing yourself to be a victim of your feelings. To act in response to these feelings will make your marriage worse, not better.

Even when only one partner is obedient to God and is willing to react lovingly and responsibly in spite of the other person's negative behavior, a marriage can be saved. In fact, this was the situation with many of the early Christians. When the Gospel first came into contact with the pagan world, not all people became Christians. Many times Christian wives were married to non-Christian Roman soldiers. Some were married to men who demanded things of their spouses that we could not even begin to imagine in our modern world. Yet Paul promised these women that their loving, Christian behavior would have an effect. If a wife responded in obedience to God toward her husband's acts—no matter how cruel—her Christian behavior would eventually wear down the spouse until he would see the power of Christ in her.

It is the same today. To a great degree, the survival of your marriage is dependent upon replacing the world's feelings/behavior model with God's feelings/obedience/ behavior model. A response to Christ in obedient love is the one thing that will make a difference. Everything else will fall miserably short.

CHAPTER FOUR

Love Is Forgiving

Many Christians recite the Lord's Prayer Sunday after Sunday, if not more often. Yet it is frightening to think that God might actually take us at our word when we pray, "Forgive us our trespasses as we forgive those who trespass against us." If God's forgiveness toward us were no more than our forgiveness toward others, a lot of us would be in real trouble.

In the last chapter we discussed the radical nature of Christian love. Christian forgiveness must be no less radical. People often say such things as, "I'll forgive, but I won't forget," or, "Just wait; I'll get even." Someone's entire life can become a collection of real or imagined wrongs done to them. Non-Christians, especially, have no working knowledge of the concept of forgiveness. Instead they carry around their resentments, all collected together in one bitter package.

For a marriage to really work, and for a Christian to get past the barriers which cause the marriage to "come unglued," there has to be a place for radical forgiveness. This concept does not come naturally nor easily to us, however.

HUMAN NATURE VS. CHRISTIAN TEACHING

Our resentments are typical of human nature untouched by Jesus Christ. We may claim to be

Christians and give declarations that our marriage is also Christian, but without forgiveness our lives contradict our claims. Without forgiveness, Christian marriage is no different than that of our non-Christian culture.

This is pretty tough medicine, but the Bible is very clear on this matter. One of the most pointed biblical passages about forgiveness is found in Matthew 18. Peter asked Jesus, "How many times shall I forgive my brother when he sins against me? Up to seven times?"

We know from other available information about Peter that he had a very volatile and temperamental personality, yet he was often the one who was most anxious to confront others with what he perceived to be unfairness or injustice. Remember that it was Peter who pulled out a sword and cut off Malchus's ear in the Garden of Gethsemane (John 18:10).

So imagine Peter wavering between his aggressive personality and the values taught by Jesus Christ. Peter knew that Jesus was requiring something of him beyond what his values demanded. Yet Peter probably wondered, *How ridiculous can this get? After all, how many times do you have to forgive a man? Seven seems like a large number and maybe even has some religious significance.* But when Peter expressed his thoughts, Jesus surprised him with His answer, "I tell you, not seven times, but seventy-seven times" (Matthew 18:22).

We aren't told of Peter's response, but he probably figured out that the issue wasn't whether Jesus meant literally 77 times. The number is much larger than seven, but it is still finite and limited. The principle Jesus was trying to share with Peter was that a Christian should not set a limit on forgiveness. We should *always* forgive.

In a marriage, the application of this principle is absolutely imperative. If a person tries to keep a private account book of marital wrongs done, the marriage is doomed. In fact, this is exactly what has already happened to many Christian marriages that are now in divorce court.

Jesus followed up his conversation with Peter by telling an interesting story:

Therefore, the kingdom of heaven is like a king who wanted to settle accounts with his servants. As he began the settlement, a man who owed him ten thousand talents was brought to him. Since he was not able to pay, the master ordered that he and his wife and his children and all that he had be sold to repay the debt.

The servant fell on his knees before him. "Be patient with me," he begged, "and I will pay back everything." The servant's master took pity on him, canceled the debt and let him go.

But when that servant went out, he found one of his fellow servants who owed him a hundred denarii. He grabbed him and began to choke him. "Pay back what you owe me!" he demanded.

His fellow servant fell to his knees and begged him, "Be patient with me, and I will pay you back."

But he refused. Instead, he went off and had the man thrown into prison until he could pay the debt. When the other servants saw what had happened, they were greatly distressed and went and told their master everything that had happened.

Then the master called the servant in. "You wicked servant," he said, "I canceled all that debt of yours because you begged me to. Shouldn't you have had mercy on your fellow servant just as I had on you?" In anger his master turned him over to the jailers to be tortured, until he should pay back all he owed.

This is how my heavenly Father will treat each of you unless you forgive your brother from your heart.
(Matthew 18:23-35)

In Jesus' day, a talent was worth about $500, and the man in the illustration owed his master 10,000 talents—about five million dollars! In those days, this much money was probably a greater amount than the whole revenue of Galilee.

When the man was unable to pay this huge sum, the master first ordered that the man, his wife, and even their children be put into forced slavery. They were also to liquidate all their personal property in order to pay the debt. But the servant asked his master for forgiveness, getting down on his knees to beg for mercy. The master took pity on the man and did something absolutely incredible—he forgave the entire debt!

Another man owed money to the man who had just been forgiven. He owed a hundred denarii—a total of about $10. But the man who was just forgiven forced this second man into servitude to pay the $10.

This parable is not just a story invented by Jesus to entertain us. He intended that it should teach us something. God, in His incredible mercy, has forgiven each one of us more than we could ever repay.

LEARNING TO FORGIVE AS WE HAVE BEEN FORGIVEN

I wonder what we would do if God demanded a just payment from us for our sins. But that's not the case. Rather, God has offered us unlimited grace and forgiveness in Jesus Christ. He then expects our forgiveness toward other people to be unlimited as well. That's why Jesus taught His followers to pray: "Forgive us our trespasses in the same way we forgive others who trespass against us."

A woman once told me, "You just don't understand, Jay. I can't forgive people that way." I reminded her of the harsh alternative. How do we dare try to claim God's all-encompassing forgiveness if we aren't willing to extend it to others? I told this woman, as I have told many others, that if we apply the standard toward ourselves that we apply toward others, we would often be in serious trouble. Whenever a person sins against us, the first thing we should do is examine our own tendency to sin in the areas of pride, arrogance, and self-justification.

Ample teachings in the Bible encourage this same principle:

"From everyone who has been given much, much will be demanded" (Luke 12:48).

"Blessed are the merciful, for they will be shown mercy" (Matthew 5:7).

"If someone forces you to go one mile, go with him two miles" (Matthew 5:41).

Another key passage that helps us understand how Christian love should differ from secular relationships is found in I John 4:19-21:

> We love because He first loved us. If anyone says, 'I love God,' yet hates his brother, he is a liar. For anyone who does not love his brother, whom he has seen, cannot love God, whom he has not seen. And He has given us this command: Whoever loves God must also love his brother.

In Matthew's Gospel this idea is expressed in Jesus' own words:

> You have heard that it was said, "Love your neighbor and hate your enemy." But I tell you: Love your enemies and pray for those who persecute you, that you may be sons of your Father in heaven. He causes his sun to rise on the evil and the good, and sends rain on the righteous and the unrighteous. If you love those who love you, what reward will you get? Are not even the tax collectors doing that? And if you greet only your brothers, what are you doing more than others? Do not even pagans do that? Be perfect, therefore, as your heavenly Father is perfect.
>
> (Matthew 5:43)

This idea of loving even our enemies is a high, radical standard. In fact, a person who has not first received God's forgiveness can't really understand or apply this principle. Someone trapped in a marriage without knowledge of this wonderful principle of forgiveness can truly be caught without hope or escape. Indeed, to overlook the principle of forgiveness is to be left without any method of bringing healing to the deep collection of resentments and hurts collected in the marriage relationship. But when a Christian knows and applies this truth to his or her marriage, then the person is capable of forgiving far beyond what others can even imagine.

Jim and Sally Conway again provide a beautiful example in their book, *Your Marriage Can Survive Mid-Life Crisis*:

> Shirley said to us, "I've been able to forgive Bruce because I love him. He has sometimes hurt me deeply, and we still have some unresolved problems, but I keep forgiving him anyway. I remember that love covers a multitude of sins; so I just put my love and forgiveness in the place of his wrongs toward me. Each time I do that it is like a fresh start on a clean sheet of paper."
>
> Forgiveness is a multifaceted gem that involves confession to God and asking His forgiveness, confession to your mate and asking his or her forgiveness, accepting God's forgiveness, accepting your mate's forgiveness, granting forgiveness to your mate, and restoring your mate through positive affirmation. Forgiveness is easier when we believe any temptation that any other person has experienced is possible in our own lives. Forgiveness is also easier to grant when we realize that we often need to be forgiven ourselves. Practicing forgiveness is easier when we realize that bitterness, hate, and grudges really have more effect on us than on our mate. The very act of withholding forgiveness keeps the bitter green juices flowing; we develop ulcers in our stomachs and lines on our faces. Forgiveness has a wonderful, releasing power not only for the other person, but also for ourselves.

I cannot say it any better. Often I've told people who are struggling with guilt in their lives that the easiest forgiveness to get is the kind that God gives. He completely understands us and our sins, yet He is willing to forgive if we confess our sins to Him. The next easiest forgiveness to get is from another person—if we humbly and honestly ask for their forgiveness and plead for their understanding. In most cases, people will be genuinely willing to forgive us and give us another chance.

THE HARDEST KIND OF FORGIVENESS

The most difficult kind of forgiveness to receive is the forgiveness we give ourselves. Often, when we have done wrong, we can get forgiveness both from God and from other people. But we punish ourselves and are filled with remorse. We believe that God and other people have forgiven us, but we forget that we need to forgive ourselves. Until we have appropriated forgiveness at *all three levels*, sin will continue to put lines on our faces and wear down our spirits.

In order to save a troubled marriage, we must have more than a secular understanding of superficial forgiveness. It is imperative to forgive *and forget*. We have to forfeit our so-called "rights" in order to apply the same standards in forgiving others that God uses for us. As we learn to do this, we develop a solid basis for rebuilding even the most difficult and troubled situations.

H. Norman Wright, in *Seasons of a Marriage* (Regal), addresses this subject when he examines one of the most difficult of all demands of forgiveness—forgiving a partner for sexual transgression:

> Once the partner has stopped the affair and has asked for forgiveness, the couple will need to spend much time in counseling and in building a new relationship. The concept that forgiveness is a process and not instantaneous must be explored as well. Forgiveness is not pretending. One cannot ignore the fact that an event has occurred. Wishing it had never occurred will not make it go away. What is done is done and being a martyr or pretending ignorance of the event does not help the relationship. In fact, a lack of confrontation and reconciliation may encourage the other person to continue or repeat the same act or behavior. Forgiveness is not a feeling. It is not a

soothing, comforting overwhelming emotional response that erases the fact from one's memory forever. It is a clear and logical action that does not bring up the past defenses and hurts, but takes each day a step at a time. Gradually there will be a bit less anger and resentment and a bit more forgiveness until, eventually, there is wholeness again. Special transgressions sometimes occur. But as with other sins, God's grace is active and the presence of Jesus Christ in a person's life can bring restoration and wholeness. It will be your choice. One of the assumptions which hinders us from forgiving and making restoration is to believe that we can control neither our memory nor our thoughts. We can choose to dwell upon the unfortunate event and the hurt which ensued, or we can focus on the repentance and restoration. If we say that we cannot get over the hurt, then we have chosen to keep it lodged in our minds. We are saying that the act is more important than the relationship with our partner. In our selective memory we can either allow the continuing oozing and festering of a cancerous, terminal sore, or we can embrace the role of a healer. Healing is more than deciding not to be angry and hurt, withdrawn or silent. Healing means reconciliation. It involves empathy, carrying the other's hurt and making it our own. It means helping the other person become whole again. Healing is a beautiful experience. It means putting into operation our original marital ambition of bringing joy, happiness, and encouragement to our partner.

Those of us who have been involved in trying to help people through marriage difficulties readily understand this process. We know that there must be a willingness on the part of the person wronged to forgive the other person and allow Christ's healing power to work. But there is greater healing and progress when *both* parties are willing to be involved in the process of forgiveness. It is a time for mutual understanding. Though one person has been caught in the transgression, the other must consider, "There but for the grace of God go I." When such love and forgiveness is at work, there is nothing that can keep the marriage from healing and growing.

ONE PERSON *CAN* MAKE A DIFFERENCE

Yet even though it is best when both parties in the marriage covenant enter into the process of forgiveness, I contend that even one determined person can make a difference. Even if only one partner is willing to forgive, that action can affect the life of the other person.

I have never taken the position that all marriages will be healed. In some situations, one party in the marriage wants out and will not listen to any appeal from his or her partner. But even in these cases we can respond in a Christian manner. We can continue to return good for evil, to love our enemies, and to do good to those who despitefully use us. Even if the marriage dissolves, God will bless us with the knowledge that we have been obedient to Him rather than reverting to our non-Christian behavior.

Christian forgiveness is backed by God's supernatural power. Just as a broken bone is often stronger after it mends, sometimes a fractured marriage (after forgiveness) will become stronger than it was before. After sin or difficulties break a marriage relationship apart, an outpouring of forgiveness from both sides can bond it again.

Many couples don't communicate well. Nor do they confront difficulties together. Often they live their married life very much on the surface. Then when real problems come, they are forced into self-examination, embarrassment, and fear of losing it all. These are the marriages that can become stronger than ever if the couples can allow Christ to have His way in their lives.

Sometimes a person will become a Christian after living a life of sin and deep alienation from God. Such a person doesn't say it was good to have lived this kind of sinful life or express a desire to go back and do it all again. Yet he or she will say, "Although I've had that experience in my past, I am grateful for it because it has taught me valuable lessons that other people have never learned." People who have experienced the bleak reality of sin can decisively turn their backs on it because they know what is involved. Others who have not gone through such a drastic learning experience will close the door on sin, but they spend their whole lives "looking through the keyhole"—perhaps even envying those who have lived lives of sinful excess.

The same is true for the married couple who has gone through deep and painful difficulties. The difficulties have a way of refining the relationship and drawing them closer—to one another, and to God. Anyone who has overcome the pain of a marriage alienated from God does not want to return to the way it was.

This outlook carries over to many kinds of struggles we go through in marriages—illness of a mate, death of a child, or the disappointment of a child's rebellion. All of these deep painful matters have the capacity to cripple and scar, but if we allow God to operate in our lives, we strengthen our relationship rather than destroy it.

WHAT MAKES A MARRIAGE 'CHRISTIAN'?

This is the assumption I think is worth repeating: a person cannot claim to have a Christian marriage if the "Christian" part of the marriage consists only of words shared at the marriage altar. The element that makes a marriage "Christian" involves the daily activity of Christ in our marriage difficulties. It includes the willingness to realize that your original commitment and covenant in marriage is worth fighting for. It requires a willingness to realize that you and your mate are caught in the midst of pain and pressure from the world around you. Together you may actually be victims of forces larger than yourselves.

We need to always remember that Christ demands obedience—a radical commitment to Him regardless of how we feel. Our obedience includes not only receiving

His forgiving love, but also passing it on to others. Yet, like Peter, we are prone to ask, "But how much is enough?"

I realize I am addressing some people who have gone through incredible pain and disappointment. Some can't find a point to their pain. Some desperately want to know when enough is enough. Others plead, "Please give me the option of saying that I've turned the other cheek and forgiven. I keep getting dumped on, and I think it's time to see a lawyer and get out of this marriage."

My answer is simple. I can't decide for you at what point your marriage ceases to be worth fighting for. Neither can anyone else. The only guideline I can provide is to act as a Christian, with the words of Christ and the teaching of the Bible to direct you.

The answer you reach may not be the one you want. But ask yourself, have you been serious about how you approach forgiveness? Have you tried to forgive in the same way that Jesus did when He forgave us so very much?

Genuine forgiveness may require extreme demands. The forgiveness that Jesus provides us required that He first go to the cross. Yet forgiveness also provides freedom and reward. And according to the author of Hebrews, the benefits far outweigh the demands:

> Therefore, since we are surrounded by such a great cloud of witnesses, let us throw off everything that hinders and the sin that so easily entangles, and let us run with perseverance the race marked out for us. Let us fix our eyes on Jesus, the author and perfecter of our faith, who for the joy set before Him endured the cross, scorning its shame, and sat down at the right hand of the throne of God. Consider Him who endured such opposition from sinful men, so that you will not grow weary and lose heart. In your struggle against sin, you have not yet resisted to the point of shedding your blood.
>
> (Hebrews 12:1-4)

This passage reminds us to look at Jesus Christ and what He went through for the sins of the world. Though He was the sinless son of God, He willingly suffered in order to forgive us. As we imitate Jesus' example of forgiveness, most of us are never required to experience actual physical abuse or death. Even though we feel that we have been wronged deeply or that we have taken as much abuse as we can, we are reminded that we have not yet come close to the depths of suffering that Jesus Christ experienced on our behalf.

I am often convicted by this passage in Hebrews. God sometimes has to remind me, "I know you feel you are persecuted and misunderstood, Jay. But Jesus *died*. You haven't gone that far yet. Are your complaints really justified?"

Of course, the answer is obvious. God expects me to behave as a Christian in obedience and forgiveness.

Corrie ten Boom was a prisoner of the Nazis during World War II, and she tells about her experience in the book, *A Prisoner and Yet* (Christian Literature Crusade). I think it is appropriate to conclude this chapter on forgiveness by quoting a pointed paragraph where she describes her time in prison:

> Shivering from cold and misery, I tried to distract my attention from my own discomfort by looking at those around me. Never in my life have I felt so wretched, so cold, so humiliated. Suddenly I remembered a painting of Jesus on Golgotha. For the first time I realized that Jesus had hung naked upon the cross. How He must have suffered! He, God's Son, whose home was heaven, and all that suffering He bore for me that I might someday go to heaven—my soul became calm within me. I felt that strength was given to me to go on.

It is precisely this kind of strength that I ask you to call upon as you try to forgive those who have so seriously caused you pain—maybe even your mate. Forgive each person even as Christ has forgiven you.

CHAPTER FIVE

Expectations and Misconceptions

Because of all the mail I receive from my radio broadcast, I think I have a fair idea of what causes people to consider divorce. One common theme in the letters I've received over the past 15 years is that people accumulate resentment due to unmet expectations. And to get a little more specific, I have categorized their comments in order of frequency to identify some issues which seem to cause the most friction.

'MARRIAGE WILL SOLVE MY PROBLEMS'

The first is stated in varying ways, but comes out something like this: "I thought marriage would solve my problems." Sometimes two people who are each only "half happy" mistakenly think they will somehow make one whole, happy unit. But what really happens is that they bring their unresolved conflicts into the marriage. So rather than the two becoming one, the degree of maladjustment compounds until each one begins blaming each other for his or her own problems.

I think married people who now find life less happy than it was before should go back to "square one." They need to examine the areas of discontent that were present in their lives prior to marriage. And they should be careful not to blame their marriage partners for failing to resolve the problem.

I can't tell you how often I've seen two unhappy people who constantly seem to irritate each other create a climate in which each person's discontent grows even faster than in the environment of singleness. If this is even remotely similar to a problem you might be facing, I believe that personal counseling with an experienced Christian counselor can be a great help to you. When we locate the source of your unhappiness, it's possible to stop blaming your marriage partner for not providing answers.

Often as we look back on our lives, we can see these things more easily. We begin to understand the pitfalls that tripped us up before—in adolescence and youth, or earlier in marriage.

'(S)HE WILL BECOME A CHRISTIAN AFTER THE WEDDING'

A second, very frequently mentioned resentment is true for both sexes, but is more common for women. That resentment is having fallen in love with a person who is not a Christian, but who had expressed interest in becoming one *before* the marriage. The problem is that *after* the marriage contract is consummated, the Christian partner loses whatever leverage she had before the wedding. No doubt this was one of the reasons behind the biblical injunction: "Do not be yoked together with unbelievers" (II Corinthians 6:14).

Major problems arise in a marriage relationship between a Christian and a non-Christian. They can reach no agreement on standards or values, much less spiritual matters. Such incompatibility is bad enough between husband and wife, but it is compounded dramatically when children become pawns in such squabbles.

The mutual physical attraction in the courtship stage rapidly fades when that's all two people have in common as they begin the real business of building a marriage. This level of incompatibility can take a heavy toll on marriages. Yet from a New Testament viewpoint, I don't believe it is reason enough to break up a marriage.

The apostle Paul reminds us that a consistent life demonstrated daily by the Christian will eventually wear down the resistance of the non-Christian partner (I Corinthians 7:12-14). Yes, there may be the need for counseling and encouragement—especially for the Christian spouse to live a consistent, loving, caring, cooperative life in front of the non-Christian partner. But the situation isn't necessarily hopeless.

'MARRIAGE WILL CHANGE MY SPOUSE'

The third most commonly shared resentment based on an unmet expectation is often stated as, "I thought marriage would change my partner." It is ridiculous and unrealistic to think of a marriage partner as we might an unfinished piece of furniture—something we will sandpaper, reshape, and finish according to our own preconceived ideas. It is true that we can all become better persons and improve our behavior toward one another. Yet our basic temperaments, values, personalities, and attitudes remain pretty much the same throughout life.

We need to be more realistic and recognize that people seldom change very much. Our goal should be to become more accepting and appreciative of the differences between each other. We can learn to be enriched by the complementary nature of a spouse's personality and gifts. The idea that we can take some sort of cookie cutter to the other person and force him or her to become what we want is destined for failure. It only brings disharmony to both people in a relationship.

'HAVING A CHILD WILL MAKE US CLOSER'

The fourth most often shared preconception is, "I thought a baby would bring us together." When you think about this, it is truly naive to think that a baby will make a capable marriage counselor. If two lives are already complicated, then bringing a third into the home will only add to the complications.

The arrival of a child brings an enormous number of demands to both the man and woman in a marriage. Yet many couples go years into a marriage wondering why the baby didn't make their life happy and solve their disagreements by bringing them closer together. It never happens that way.

'MARRIAGE WILL BE DIFFERENT FOR US'

Another theme that comes through our radio mail is: "I thought our marriage would be different than others." Somehow, almost every young dating couple comes to the conclusion that their love alone will see them through any obstacle. They see the stresses and strains in their parents' marriages and in their friends' relationships, and figure there is something wrong with those people. As they talk and plan for their own marriage, they conclude that other people are not as strong as they are. They truly believe that *this* marriage will be different.

There is a wonderful quality to dating, and a marvelous joy in looking into someone's eyes with love and affection. This is a unique feeling—that two people have a truly special relationship and a great love that supersedes all others. But that's all it is—a *feeling*.

We are somehow able to suspend reality during a dating relationship. Reality would tell us that another autonomous human being has his or her own set of personality traits, aspirations, and desires. We shouldn't expect to enter a relationship and miraculously expect our own personality quirks to instantly merge with the other person's into a single harmonious relationship without any stress or strain. The truth is, everyone goes through periods of adjustment in marriage. No matter how special the dating relationship, courtship, and bond of love has been in the past, adjustment in marriage is not achieved simply through hope. It takes hard work, forgiveness, patience, and more.

'TWO CAN LIVE AS CHEAPLY AS ONE'

In one form or another, an additional theme that runs throughout my mail is, "I didn't know marriage would cost so much." The old cliché that two can live as cheaply as one has deceived many couples. Perhaps a horse and a sparrow, as two creatures, can live as cheaply as one horse alone. But the maxim doesn't hold true for human beings. Harsh financial demands are placed on couples and families. The idea that marriage will somehow alleviate the problem often causes terrible arguments over finances. In fact, money problems—how much we are going to spend or save and what are we going to spend it on—are among the most serious problems in most marriage relationships.

Can Misperceptions Be Overcome?

I have listed only some of the most common resentments and expectations from my mail. But there are many other things over which people will seek a divorce. You may even have your own list. At this point, however, I ask, "Can your Christian commitment overcome misconceptions and resentments caused by unmet expectations?"

My answer is "Yes! Most assuredly, yes!" But this is true only if we are willing to give up our misconceptions as false and immature ideas. Maybe we were unrealistic, immature, or stubborn in relationship to the Bible, our parents, our advisers, or common sense. If we see evidence of this and confront the problem, then we can work on the issues that actually divide us.

The other option is to simply continue to whine and come up with excuses for why marriage isn't working out. But in that case, we never get to a solution. Isn't it better to admit that we are already in the midst of a marriage and that we have made a commitment to another person in God's presence? Then we can work through our problems. Sometimes we may also need to admit that we cannot make it on our own. And if that's the case, there are pastors, marriage counselors, and Christian friends who can help us. From their experience, they'll know how to solve some of our problem issues.

'We Fight Over Roles and Responsibilities'

Another category of problems consistently shows up in my mail. In addition to hearing about people's basic misconceptions, I also hear from Christians who feel trapped in a marriage that is full of problems and headed for divorce court. Most of their comments express a tremendous dissatisfaction over roles and responsibilities in marriage.

In an earlier chapter we already discussed how, in modern culture, people often base their self-worth on vocational or professional accomplishments. It is virtually impossible for some people to talk to one another without constantly referring to the way they earn their living. Add to that problem the fact that many women feel that men have an unfair dominance both in the home and in the workplace.

Feminist literature has caused many women to question the justice and validity of the male as head of the home. Even Christian couples go through a great deal of ambivalence and heated discussion on this subject. Women, quite justifiably, want meaning in their lives. In a vocation-oriented culture, this is interpreted in terms of power, importance, and reward. Personal value is often measured by position, professional accomplishment, and remuneration.

The illusion is that power, importance, and reward bring fulfillment and happiness. But it is only an illusion. Women drawn to such an illusion should learn from the example of many men who have historically struggled to attain these goals, yet remained unhappy. Value, self-worth, and meaning are imputed to us—both male and female—by God.

According to Genesis 1:27, "God created man in His own image, in the image of God He created him; male and female He created them." The word "man" used in this verse does not refer to the male gender only, but mankind as a whole. God made mankind in His own image, male and female.

I realize the danger of saying this without further explanation, but I think there is a sense in which God is female as well as male. It may well be that this is why, when two become one in a marriage, they have insights into God's character and attributes that they didn't see previously. But it is not the marriage itself that brings out these insights.

A bullish, insensitive, married man will not know more about God than a thoughtful, sensitive, unmarried man. But a thoughtful, sensitive, married man in a relationship of mutual trust and respect with an equally caring wife will know more about God than he could ever have known without marriage. Nevertheless, many couples struggle deeply, never really seeing through the illusion that human value is attached to professional accomplishment.

Frequently there is a "flip side" to this problem having to do with the concept of *submission* based on Ephesians 5:22-24:

> Wives, submit to your husbands as to the Lord. For the husband is the head of the wife as Christ is the head of the church, His body, of which He is the Savior. Now as the church submits to Christ, so also wives should submit to their husbands in everything.

God never intended that the concept of submission should be used as a device to keep wives in subjection or to give husbands arbitrary and capricious power over their spouses. Instead, the apostle Paul sums up God's intention as one in which a husband's love should parallel the love of Christ for the church. The husband's role is stated simply and clearly, and allows little room for misinterpretation. It is a lifetime challenge that does not permit an air of superiority from a husband toward a wife, even though the wife is to be submissive to the husband.

'I'M TOO TIRED'

Another source of fractures in the marriage bond is physical fatigue among women. Not only does my radio mail illustrate this, but others tell me the same thing. Dr. James Dobson considers it a serious problem—especially for young wives. Childbearing takes a great toll on the woman. And as if that responsibility were not enough, today's wives and mothers often have a full-time job outside the home.

Sometimes the husband seems insensitive to the fact that a working wife not only has to carry the responsibilities of job, children, and family, but also do the cooking, cleaning, and other homemaking as well. That's a volatile mixture, indeed, which cannot be neutralized until the man either observes his wife's near collapse or is directed to a marriage workshop or counselor.

It is amazing how often men are blind to the unfairness of this situation. Usually the problem is not intended injustice on the part of the husband—just ignorance. In such cases, there is no better solution than a simple, straightforward confrontation by the wife. She must acquaint her Christian husband with the injustice of this common situation.

On the other hand, men encounter problems with fatigue and stress as well. Many men feel their wives don't understand the pressures they face in their workplace. Career demands in men also add to our list of reasons for marital breakdowns.

Most men involved in extramarital affairs are not primarily involved for sexual reasons, as was said earlier. Rather, they are on a quest for understanding, appreciation, and affirmation. When wives give most of their time and attention to children and housekeeping, men sometimes feel used. They imagine that their only value is as a breadwinner, and in many cases they feel unappreciated.

STOP AND REEVALUATE

In modern marriage relationships, it seems wise for Christian couples to back off a step or two and try to understand each other's needs. Women need the support and help of their husbands both in the child-rearing and homemaking tasks. There is nothing unmanly in being fair about work around the home. Conversely, a man shouldn't have to work every day at his job and feel that his own spouse is unappreciative.

These are simple adjustments to make. If husband and wife discuss them together now, they might avoid talking with a stranger later in a law office or divorce court.

These expectations, misconceptions, and insensitivities that I have related are not of such serious complexity that they need to destroy our marriages. Yet a marriage situation will only grow worse if they are ignored, or perhaps added to someone's pride or inability to forgive. Every married person needs to make a serious commitment to work through any problem before it can become a source of destruction for the relationship that God holds most sacred in all of society.

By way of reminder, Christian people have available not only their own godly wisdom and strength, but also the added power of the Holy Spirit. It is this supernatural quality that helps us to be more patient, understanding, fair, and forgiving. We have the power to solve problems that destroy other marriages and families. Destructive cycles can be broken and our marriages can be healed. But you have to be willing to *act*. Once you know what problems you need to confront, ask God for the courage and patience to *do* it.

CHAPTER SIX

Male and Female Differences

I have sat with countless people and listened as they expressed their frustrations concerning the sexual aspect of marriage. Though not every conversation pertains to sex, the topic is mentioned so often that I have come to believe it is a widespread problem in marriage relationships. And after contrasting the comments of men with those of women, some specific issues come to light.

WHAT MEN SAY

Men who complain about their sexual lives almost universally say that the frequency and intensity of their sexual relationship is less than they expected. A common complaint is: "I'm disappointed, I guess. Sure, my wife fulfills her role as a sex partner—when I ask. But I get a feeling of despair over the fact that she makes me feel that I'm some kind of a panting animal asking for something that's really not spiritual or legitimate for a mature man—let alone a Christian man."

Some men express tremendous problems with their fantasy lives. According to one man, "I have the usual male sexual desires. I want some variety, even to the point where I have desires for women other than my wife. But I've learned to live dutifully within the constraints of my wife's sexual appetites."

WHAT WOMEN SAY

When I listen to the wives of these men, I hear them saying, "I can't believe my husband's attitude! Sex is all he thinks about. It's always on his mind and he tends to see me only as a sex object. He doesn't want anything to do with me after he has finished with the sex act."

Male/female differences are more complex than can be defined and explained in a single book, much less this chapter. It is clear that sexual tensions between husband and wife can affect the success of a marriage. And on a very practical level, we need to develop some generalizations to help spouses understand and accept each other so the tension can be alleviated.

DOING WHAT COMES NATURALLY?

Indeed, many women see their husbands as some kind of brute who doesn't really care about the subtleties of female sexual interest. It seems that sex between husband and wife would be a matter of "doin' what comes naturally." Yet what comes naturally to one may not seem natural for another.

Still, I have to smile sometimes when couples come to me with this problem. It wasn't always like this for them. A natural uniformity of sexual appetite was present at one time. A common sexual interest existed during their adolescence—maybe in the backseats of automobiles, in parks, or at other places where young people kissed, necked, and otherwise expressed desire for each other. But somehow, after the first blush of marriage, some people develop great tension over the subject of sex.

Over the years I have begun to see general consistencies among the feelings of women toward men and men toward women. For the man, the desire for sex is triggered in the eye or imagination—what he sees or what he fantasizes. But for the woman, the desire for sex seems to originate more often in the mind or touch—through a caress, a gentle embrace, thoughts of security, a feeling of deep abiding love, words of tenderness, or a quiet intimate moment.

SEX AND TIMING

The man is quickly aroused sexually. He can experience heightened sexual stimulation repeatedly and rapidly. The woman is aroused much more slowly, but she reaches a higher peak in her arousal. Women rise on a slow, continuous curve of sexual arousal and climax, then are slow to come down from stimulation. As the peak of arousal diminishes, wives enjoy the intimacy of cuddling and feeling secure.

The man's desire is like a brushfire that flares up quickly and suddenly dies out. The woman is like a flame within the trunk of a tree that burns with deep, glowing embers for a long period of time.

For the man, sex tends to be an event that begins, takes place, and ends within a particular fashion. The woman thinks more in terms of sexuality as a relationship—something which lasts for a long time.

The woman's desire might begin as she thinks warm thoughts when her husband says nice things to her at the end of his workday. She is aroused by hearing his thoughts over dinner and by his quiet touches, hugs, and assurances throughout the evening. As she puts the children to bed, the distractions and demands are gone. She can relax and give herself over to a time of sexual pleasure. All these things her husband has done have provided a prelude to her desire and sexuality.

But the man, although loving and thoughtful, tends to also be busy about various activities. He reads the paper, watches ball games on TV and then, two minutes after the last field goal is kicked, he is ready to think of sex. This contrast in approaches to sexuality brings about tremendous difficulties of timing.

SEX AND PHYSIOLOGY

The man's sex organs are external to his body and don't seem to deeply affect his inner life. The woman's sex organs are internal and seem to affect her at a much deeper human level. Inhibitions, distractions, and anything else that affects a woman's whole person also greatly affect her sexual stimulation.

This may be one of the reasons why fantasy is more predominant in male sexual expression. Men can be stimulated externally. Woman experience sexuality within.

SEX AND PERFORMANCE

For men, overt sexuality often becomes a standard of manliness. In our society, sexual performance can be perceived as an extension of life performance or a substitute for potency in job or career.

This is why I previously stated that very few adulterous relationships have anything to do with sexuality. Yes, they almost always relate to impotence, but not *sexual* impotence. The person involved feels impotent in life and even misunderstood by his wife. He then thinks he has to go out and prove his manliness through sexual activity. Sometimes he even becomes a sexual athlete as a way to overcome his perceived impotence regarding his career.

For the woman, sexuality is not an extension of competence. Sexuality cannot be separated from the rest of her being. When sex is approached as a performance or something external, it affects her self-esteem and she feels used.

SEX AND COMMUNICATION

Another problem is that many men intend sex as a form of communication. The husband feels that he is expressing his love toward his wife through sexual activity. But very few women are satisfied to communicate only through sex. They need verbal communication and reassurance. Before they are ready for sexual activity, they want to hear words of endearment and love.

Many men are surprised to learn that great numbers of women testify to feeling fulfilled just by touches and caresses that don't lead to actual sexual intercourse. Men can't believe that this is fulfilling for women, because it's certainly not enough for their own sexual appetites. For them, the climax of sexual release is the crowning achievement. Anything less tends to be a buildup and then disappointment. Sometimes the man even uses sex for simple (and perhaps irresponsible) release of sexual tension—a momentary abandonment of his cares and worries. But for the woman, sex is never trivial.

SEX AND THE FEAR OF CONCEPTION

Another matter that affects women more than men is the possibility of conception. Despite modern birth control methods, the woman often fears sex at a subliminal level. Since the time of Eve, women have had to deal with the realities of conception.

It doesn't simply create concern for a woman before her marriage; it continues after the wedding. Conception is often an inhibiting factor in a woman's sexuality because of the complexities and involvements of childbearing. The old joke is true: "If the husbands were the ones to get pregnant and have babies, humans would become extinct by the next generation." So the husband needs to be understanding of his wife's subliminal apprehension or inhibitions in this matter.

SEX AND AFFIRMATION

While the husband tries to understand his wife and the wife tries to understand her husband, neither one can "overdo" affirmation for the other. Most men need affirmation not only about their sexual prowess, but about their life competency as well. Women desire affirmation about their personality, beauty, and the things that reinforce stability and security. For women, insecurity is often caused by fear that they might lose their partners through death or infidelity.

Men tend to lead with their thoughts, live a somewhat analytical life, and express their feelings only after logical thought processes. For most women, life is experienced first through feelings, then intuitions, and finally their thoughts are organized into coherent patterns. Through the ages, women's intuition has seemed almost like a sixth sense for mankind because women are so good at this feeling.

Men tend to think in broad generalities. They draw a picture of life with huge, bold strokes across the canvas, like a Picasso abstract painting. The woman tends to see life in terms of specifics. Her canvas is much more detailed, like a Leonardo da Vinci painting, where each small feature is important and stands out from the others.

When the husband gets home, the wife wants to hear about his day. But he is already tired of those details and wants to think about other things. In general, men tend to be more goal-oriented and driven toward achievement. Women think more deeply and are more process-oriented. As such, women are concerned not just with the destination, but also with what happens along the way.

SEX AND TERMINOLOGY

For men, sexuality is often associated with words like "possession," "aggression," "frustration," "potency," "manliness," and "macho." These are action words that drive toward purposeful goals. A woman's list of words of sexuality contain softer expressions—"security," "caring," "protection," "loving," or "loyalty." These words don't look like arrows on a piece of paper. They look more like clouds—something to rest in.

These ideas and mental pictures about male/female differences have come to me from specific conversations with real people involved in marriage struggles. My purpose for sharing them with you is that, as these men and women shared their thoughts with me, they also provided general characteristics about male/female differences. In a marriage situation, it is imperative that each understands the other. Otherwise, what the husband desires as an expression of love can appear to the wife as disgusting or degrading demands.

BE AWARE OF THESE DIFFERENCES

I feel our greatest help can come from recognizing the simple distinctives that make us different. So before you find yourself thinking that your marriage has totally failed, that somehow your relationship as husband and wife is at an end, you need to find hope. I think that hope comes from understanding that these male/female characteristics are natural. They have developed as a result of culture and environment over a period of years (going back to when man was the hunter/gatherer/ warrior and woman was the nurturer/childbearer/keeper of the hearth).

Nevertheless, we bring these characteristics and differences into our marriages. To change these attitudes would require generations of conditioning and change. So in the meantime, the most important task for husbands and wives is that of trying to love one another, to value our male/female differences, and in the name of the Lord Jesus Christ to give up our individual prerogatives in favor of the well-being of our partners.

As a young engaged man, I had some apprehension about the honeymoon and what might be expected of me as a new husband. I devoured all the information I could get on the subject. I got the necessary books and studied the diagrams, pictures, and descriptions that I thought would help me. I also asked the advice of a close friend who had married a year before. He was a sincere Christian who shared my views about God and Christian marriage. In retrospect, I find his advice to still be the best I have ever heard—better than that found in the hundreds of articles, technical papers, and psychological books that I have read on this subject. My friend simply said, "Jay, just forget about yourself."

This advice is the key to sexual adjustment within marriage. In fact, God has chosen to bestow opposite but complementary characteristics to make the sexual union so wonderful and pleasurable. If you think about the fulfillment of your partner rather than attempting to "get something" from the other person, your marriage will take on new meaning.

Jesus told His followers, "Whoever finds his life will lose it, and whoever loses his life for My sake will find it" (Matthew 10:39). We receive new life as we give ("lose") our lives to Jesus. And to a degree, the same principle is true in all areas of life. If you are willing to submerge your personal concerns on behalf of your partner, then in some miraculous sense the biblical promise comes true for you. Whenever you choose to "lose your life" for another person, God gives it back to you. In the process, He also provides you the deepest satisfaction and fulfillment.

Naturally, you can expect problems to arise in a marriage where neither party is willing to give to the other. If a basically selfish male is married to a basically selfish female, and if each thinks of sex as a way to get something from the other, they will both be disappointed. It is impossible to receive satisfaction, pleasure, fulfillment, or security without the biblical process of yielding.

If I demand my "rights," then I'm pretty much like my grandmother's old orange juice extractor. I just keep on taking from and squeezing the other person until she turns into a dry and empty pulp. If both partners are squeezing each other, then these two empty rinds will soon discover that marriage is not the wonderful, fulfilling experience that it was promised to be. Instead, it turns out to be something dry, empty, and totally unfulfilling.

A Christian couple needs to believe that God created them the way they are for a reason. They must realize that an understanding of each other's differences can revitalize their relationship. As Christians, even if they are practicing unbridled selfishness, they can transform sexuality from a divider of relationships into a godly gift. With a little work, they can again come to see sex as God intended it—a one-of-a-kind experience that will bring them closer together.

CHAPTER SEVEN

Maturity Is Not Monotony

When I studied about Ponce de Leon in school, I remember thinking that it was ridiculous that anyone would devote so much effort searching for a "fountain of youth." At the time I thought of his huge expeditions as being so much medieval foolishness. But I've changed my mind since then. Knowledgeable people in the 20th century pursue this same mythical illusion with even greater commitment.

With the advances of modern science and the tremendous improvements in public health and diet, today's people live longer and enjoy their health much later into life. They still grow old and eventually die, yet society itself seems to be in a state of denial concerning this reality. Our culture has put such an emphasis on youth and health that you'd think old age is some sort of disease. Anything connected with the aging process is to be avoided at all costs.

BEHIND THE ALLURE OF YOUTH AND BEAUTY

You've probably seen the glamorous advertisements with mothers and daughters displayed in bathing suits, where you are supposed to guess which is the teenage daughter. Our cultural goal seems to be for all mothers to look as young as their daughters. But of all people, Christians should be capable of identifying the absurdity of this pursuit as well as the threat that such a concept presents to the ultimate plan of God.

The blossom of a plant is the part that looks beautiful in a bouquet, yet has little functional value. Its real purpose is to attract insects to pollinate from flower to flower. The blossom is only "fulfilled" when it eventually loses its petals and produces a seed or a fruit. It is the bearing of fruit that propagates the plant and assures the continuance of the species.

The same is true of human beings. We may certainly enjoy seeing a beautiful, young body. We might even admire the ease with which younger people can respond to physical challenges. Yet we must understand that old age is not a junkyard, but rather a goal toward which the blossom of youth heads. People become fruitful through experience and wisdom, and they pass their insights to future generations. An obsession with youth and self-preoccupation is diametrically opposed to the basic tenets and goals of the Christian faith.

People mature, grow older, and die. The cycle of life is inevitable. But we shouldn't equate maturity with monotony, nor old age with tedium and uselessness. Marriage cannot be all honeymoon. Indeed, it would be pretty boring if it were.

Marriages that constantly try to focus on youth and youthful activity are destined for failure. It is this kind of obsession that has coined a new term for our generation—the so-called *mid-life crisis*. Men and women who come to their middle-age years often have deep anxieties and regrets because they feel their youth has passed them by. In my work I often talk with a number of men (or the wives of men) in mid-life crisis. They are unable to come to terms with their advancing age—especially in light of the media hype reminding them of the importance of youth in our culture.

MID-LIFE'S EFFECT ON BOTH SEXES

Men at middle age jokingly talk about trading in their 40-year-old wives for two 20 year olds. I tell them, "You're not wired for 220. You'll only end up playing the fool and disobeying God." Unfortunately, on a more serious level, I've seen how difficult it is for many men to resist the temptation to reject their "old" wives for younger women.

TV commercials show vigorous, well-muscled, self-assured, young men sitting around a campfire after hunting, fishing, playing football, or some other active pursuit. A lot of male viewers imagine sitting there and hearing, "It doesn't get any better than this!" (Seldom do the men stop to ask what "it" is.) But in the face of such fantasy and tease, it's almost impossible for today's men not to reject maturity in favor of this elusive fountain of youth.

And don't think this mid-life crisis applies only to men. More than one husband has confided to me about how his wife, after the kids were grown, left him for a younger man. One husband described how his wife started going to the health club to work out. The exercises helped her regain a more youthful, sensual, and exciting body. She also regained her self-confidence and self-esteem. So what did she do with her newfound assets? She abandoned her husband for someone else.

It is possible for anyone to get caught in this trap. But Christian couples should have the help of God's Word and a heightened understanding of His purposes. They should be capable of seeing beyond the visual illusions of Madison Avenue. They should move on to the deeper stuff of life. And when they decide to resist the temptations put forth by the secular media, they will also discover marriage in its most satisfying and fulfilling form.

BEWARE THE MEDIA BIAS

We can no longer expect the secular media to reflect a Christian or Judeo-Christian worldview as they once did. Today the world's values usually stand in opposition to Christianity. Educators and theologians can give you the background of how and when things changed. But Western media has presented this bias long enough to convince even Christians of its secular-humanist, hedonistic worldview. This standard is so universal and pervasive that nearly everyone takes it for granted. We rarely bother to question the ethics, values, or morals of what we see, hear, or read anymore. Yet a person who lives his or her life looking in a rearview mirror is a rather pathetic picture.

We are all bombarded with youthful images and are forced to struggle with their influence. Mothers try to look the age of their daughters. A man sees his television counterpart romantically running down a pier with a woman half his age. The well-built man and the lithe girl jump through the air in one fluid motion onto the deck of a yacht. While they are still in the air, the man unfastens the rope on the pier with one uninterrupted, coordinated move. The two of them disappear into the cabin of the yacht, which speeds off into the sunset for the couple's implied sexual marathon.

Any couple who plans to have a solid and lasting marriage will have to rid themselves of these foolish, youth-obsessed stereotypes. Otherwise, the now familiar mid-life crisis will eventually hit them. And when those symptoms hit, they hurt. Their pitiful, foolish behavior eventually drives them to divorce court.

THE POSITIVE ELEMENTS OF MATURITY

We need to dispel the myth that maturity is the beginning of the end and that getting older is to be avoided at all costs. Youth should be an attractive time for us, but we must remember that it is transient. If we allow it to become an ideal, it opposes the genuine, deep relationships that God intends us to have.

The apostle Paul said, "When I became a man, I put childish ways behind me" (I Corinthians 13:11). Such a comment requires a great deal of faith for many of us. But God knows what He is doing. As we mature, He enhances our fulfillment and joy. It's not His purpose to take away our satisfaction with life as we grow older.

As we mature, we discover lasting truths that bring true satisfaction. For example, a mature person accepts responsibility for his or her acts. We no longer blame others for our problems. We begin to understand and accept the realities of cause and effect. We learn that life consists of both pain and pleasure. We find that the TV fairy-tale life is just a fantasy. And as mature people, we can accept ourselves for what God has made us to be, realizing that criticism of this "self" is criticism of God.

Maturity also demands that we begin to accept others in the same way we accept ourselves. We realize that everyone is unique, and we can accept their diversity. The inability to accept diversity is a form of arrested development and represents a lack of mature thinking.

We also stop wishing that we were something we never could be. Realistically, only a few guys earn high school letter sweaters. Only a handful of girls are cheerleaders or homecoming queens. If we didn't achieve all our desires when we *were* young, why should we expect to do it now?

We need to come to terms with that fact that God makes people in all sizes and shapes, and with varying talents and abilities. But one thing God does not create is bad work. He has made us with differing gifts, but they are all equally important and necessary. Our ultimate worth is imputed to us by God. All other approaches to self-worth are shallow, artificial, cosmetic, or false.

When our more mature understandings are applied to our marriages, we can begin to lay the groundwork for a truly deep and solid relationship that can keep us from the fickle and fruitless searching for perfection. We also begin to understand the importance of trust. No longer are we so insecure that we become jealous of every interest that a spouse develops that is new to us. We are able to allow our spouses to grow independently without being smothered by our insecurity and fear.

A mature person learns to accept reality. The immature person sees himself or herself standing on the stage of some soap opera—acting out a melodrama, always feeling martyred or misunderstood, and longing to be the hero or heroine of every plot. A mature person seeks objectivity in every relationship with other persons, and refuses to soak in self-delusion. He or she believes that it is always better to deal in facts, realizing that manipulation of truth is unproductive.

A TIME TO EXPAND YOUR HORIZONS

When a couple commits themselves to reject the "youth myth" and accepts the joy, adventure, and excitement of maturity, they are able to enjoy the benefits of marriage at a level that is hardly known by today's couples. We grow together as persons and begin to see our mutual dreams come to life. But spending time together in mutual pursuits doesn't just happen! Such compatibility has to be cultivated and nurtured. We must learn to enjoy each other's interests.

Women must learn to enjoy going to sports events, and men need to learn to appreciate concerts and museums. One person might need to give up participation on the church softball team for a mutual involvement in things like golf or tennis that two can do for the enjoyment of being together.

I recognize that married people live in two different worlds—either they have two different careers, or one works in the workplace and the other at home. If they aren't careful, they can be separated by their divergent interests. To avoid this potential problem, Jane and I began to cultivate things that we could do together. We found that one of the most wonderful things available to bring us together as a couple is intellectual compatibility. We read books "together." I'll read the book, then she'll read it, and then we discuss it. We are constantly involved together in a wide-ranging world of ideas and situations. We read things that stretch us and cause us to know each other's position on issues. This brings us alive intellectually and teaches us to respect one another. We also learn a great deal by this experience.

When we attend plays or movies, we try to go out afterward, sit down over coffee and pie, and share our opinions of the performance with each other. In such experiences, we are drawn closer together. We look for new cultural experiences in music and art, knowing that they cause us to grow.

Where does it say that someone only grows intellectually when he is age 15 to 25? Actually, the growth curve can accelerate as we are older and have more money and time for new adventures, nature, walks, exercise, and travel. These mature activities are of infinitely greater satisfaction than the simple nibbling of each other's earlobes in the backseat of an automobile.

Another way to enhance mature marriages is through family interests. Continuing a relationship with children is even more rewarding when they are young adults rather than toddlers who need to be diapered, fed, and watched every minute. I can't begin to tell you how meaningful and satisfying it is to have children who are also close friends with whom we can interact and share experiences. Such rewards are simply not available to people who insist on immaturity in regard to commitment to marriage and family.

There are other tremendous rewards available as we mature in our marriages with compatible friends of about the same age and interests. I remember watching the film *Cocoon* with two other couples. The film was about a group of old people who were caught up in a science fiction event that would keep them alive virtually forever. The six of us went out for coffee and dessert afterward and discussed the film. As I looked at our group, I said, "Isn't it interesting how we are all growing older? Our children are grown and here we are—three couples, and all good friends."

The others agreed. Then someone said, "Let's make a commitment, a covenant to grow old together."

Another person added, "We could care for one another and protect each other from becoming the kind of people who simply grow old and bitter, who withdraw into themselves."

We discussed the idea some more and decided to commit ourselves to the kind of friendship that will stimulate and challenge each other intellectually, to involvement in volunteer work and service, and to find ways to use our experience for the good of the people around us.

This conversation has resulted in a relationship that has been a tremendous source of energy, enjoyment, and spiritual blessing to each of us. We consult with one another at every turn in our lives. We wouldn't think of doing things without involving the others.

Such relationships are rewards that take place only after struggling through some of the stages of immaturity in a marriage. And believe me, for the Christian couple, they're worth fighting for!

FROM FRUSTRATION TO FULFILLMENT

Almost all marriages go through several stages of development. The early romantic courtship stage is filled with idealism and ignorance. The honeymoon stage is where we attempt to say everything through love and sexuality while building "a love nest for two." Then, almost inevitably, there is a period of disillusionment and boredom. We wonder, as in the Peggy Lee ballad, "Is That All There Is?"

Sometimes we even go through periods of separation. It may be only the isolation of trying to work through our lives on our own, losing ourselves in hobbies, sports, increased time on the job, or the demands of home and children. Or maybe the separation is more than emotional, as one of the partners leaves.

In either situation, we find ourselves feeling trapped, wondering what life is really all about. But as those problems are worked through, the final stage of the marriage relationship can be mature love and commitment.

I've counseled enough couples to know that virtually everyone goes through each of these various stages of marriage at one time or another. For the couples who will see it through, who finally arrive at the stage of mature love, they can look at each other and say, "Let's forget the other stages—they're only illusions. Let's give up the myths. Let's refuse to permit ourselves to separate—either emotionally or physically. As Christians, let's believe that true love involves seeking the well-being of one another no matter what it costs. Let's apply the love of Christ to our marriage. Let's see what will happen if we really take Christianity seriously in our relationship."

If you'll do this, I'm convinced from my own experience that maturity is not monotony. In fact, it is the key that opens the door toward true fulfillment.

CHAPTER EIGHT

The Courtship Restored

T hink back for a moment to your high school biology class, as your teacher used the ever-popular example of a frog to explain the nature of cold-blooded creatures. (In most cases this experiment is explained verbally rather than demonstrated.) No frog in its right mind would willingly hop into a pan of very hot water. Yet it's possible to put a frog in a pot of cold water on a stove and *slowly* heat the water. The frog doesn't feel the changes as they take place. Its body adjusts to the heating water, and the frog doesn't realize it is in danger. In fact, if done slowly enough, the frog will be cooked without even knowing what has happened.

The same is true, too often, in deteriorating relationships. Most marriage trouble doesn't take place suddenly. Rather, problems develop almost imperceptibly over a long period of time. Events begin to occur which would be obvious danger signals under normal conditions. But when they happen very, very slowly, people sometimes begin to endure things that are abnormal or even sinful—things for which they have no business getting into.

THE RIGHT PERSON THE FIRST TIME

We must not allow this gradual influence of problems to cloud our thinking. A Chicago divorce attorney has observed, "Most people marry the right person the first time." I agree that most people (in the courtship process) understand intuitively how human relations work and usually start off on the right foot. We enjoy the company of the one we love and try to find creative ways to be with that person.

The purpose of this chapter is to help you rethink your own courtship and restore your courtship experience (with a little effort and self-discipline). Keep in mind what a warm and delightful experience it was to be in love. You could hardly wait for your wedding day. In all likelihood, those around you were even a little embarrassed because of your preoccupation with the other person.

Yet after starting out so well, something happens. That "something" is the enemy of relationships. It might be described as "taking each other for granted." Somehow, we forget that the person with whom we have decided to share our life is still special and deserves the same attention which took place during courtship.

What was so special about youthful courtship? Why was it so satisfying and intense? If you can recall those pleasurable characteristics, you should be encouraged to restore the courtship missing from your troubled marriage.

But before we examine these qualities, I would like to remind you of the biblical principle briefly mentioned in Chapter 6—the concept that as we "lose" our life we actually find it, and that if we try too hard to find life and hold on to it, we eventually lose it. This principle is central to all happy and fulfilling human relationships. Though it refers specifically to our relationships with God, it also works in relationship to one another.

All good courtships reflect this type of selflessness. The couple acts in ways that show special care and thoughtfulness. Small gestures prevent them from feeling taken for granted. The young man is quick to open the door for his lover. He looks out for her and shows his thoughtfulness. She is quick to discover what he likes and to do things that please him. But when people live together for a while, they often begin to take each other for granted as they become thoughtless and careless about the other. Both begin to overlook opportunities to show love in their relationship.

PUBLIC AFFIRMATION

I've heard from countless couples who are on the verge of divorce. One of the most common complaints I hear from wives is, "He treats me decently enough in public, but he doesn't treat me nearly as well in private."

This, of course, provides a clue that courtesy is connected to a person's will. When we are around people who expect good behavior, we can flip a mental switch and turn on our best behavior. And when we're alone, we can just as easily turn it off and return to our inconsiderate selfishness. Too many Christians treat their spouses in a careless, shoddy, unthoughtful, or discourteous manner.

I believe if a person can be civil and caring in public, then he or she is perfectly capable of doing the same in private. Restored courtships will involve the restoration of courtesy—a renewed concern for the other person's feelings, opinions, and desires. It's amazing how much stronger a man's marriage gets when he learns to respond to questions with, "Well, I'll have to ask my wife. I want to get her opinion on this issue." This simple courtesy and others like it will begin to pay dividends in restoring courtship relations.

When a person is willing to "give up" his or her life by abandoning personal prerogatives in favor of the mate's, something miraculous happens. Life becomes fulfilled and we suddenly find we are receiving the very things that we thought we had abandoned. God gives them to us "pressed down, shaken together and running over" (Luke 6:38).

Most people who are in love practice this kind of selflessness and preoccupation with the other person's well-being (without even realizing it). As they do, they experience a wonderful and exciting chapter of their life. Poets describe such selfless love as something that strikes like lightning, or as some strange and magical mood that overcomes us. Pragmatists tell us it's simply the result of certain behavior toward another human being.

My contention is that poetry should take a backseat to practicality. I believe that selfless love is a choice and that such behavior definitely gets results. That means love can be rekindled! Genuine excitement and spontaneity can be restored in anyone's life, if we will only discipline ourselves to do the important "little" things that once came so naturally.

Granted, your *feelings* of love may have died, almost imperceptibly, like our frog on the stove. But courtship can be rekindled. Maybe it's been a long time since you were at the courtship stage of your relationship. If so, let's refresh your memory with some of the things that made it so special.

EXCLUSIVITY IN COURTSHIP

What does courtship look like? First, there is the characteristic that I call focus or exclusivity. When a person is in love, he or she has a steady concentration on the other person. The wedding ceremony includes this element in the vow to "forsake all others."

Can you remember your high school days when Friday or Saturday night came along and you had to have a date? Most of the events required couples, so you would probably go through your list of school friends to find someone. But when that special person came along, you no longer needed your list. In fact, if you couldn't date the one you were in love with, you would probably prefer to stay home. You simply could not be satisfied going without that special person.

During courtship, your life became totally focused on that one individual. No event was complete or worthwhile without that person who brought true happiness. So are those days over? No. It is still possible for you to focus your exclusivity of concentration on one person, just as you did during courtship.

Too often other things creep into your life. For one thing, time is spent away from that person on the job, where your energies are zapped and you come dragging home without the strength to do things together. Other times you focus on your children. It's easy for kids to become the center of a person's life. But even though they are dear to you, they can innocently rob you of your courtship relationship, causing your marriage to lose its sense of exclusivity.

This brings up the subject of priorities. I am regularly asked, "How does a Christian make a priority list?" I sometimes surprise people. They expect me to say, "First of all, put God at the top of your list." That sounds like the right thing to do as a Christian.

Yet in my thinking, that is not the way to do it. Technically, God should not be listed apart from anyone else on your hierarchy, but rather should permeate every relationship. But for purposes of understanding, let's put God at the top of the list. In second place, I put Myself. Someone might say, "Well, it seems that Others should be before Myself." But unless you have control of your own self-life, you cannot give your "Self" away to other people. So the relationship you enjoy with God has to prepare you for relationships with others. If your "Self" does not exist, then you cannot give of your "Self," and your "Self" can't serve others.

So for the priority list, let me simply say that God and my relationship with God are together at the top. Next I list Spouse, followed by Children. Some people would list Family instead, observing that Spouse and Children should go together. But I make a distinction and separate Spouse from Family because of what I said earlier—often there are times in a marriage where the spouse gets lost in the shuffle. It is easy for a husband and wife to start to see each other in their parental roles rather than as individuals with real, personal needs.

In the rekindling of a courtship, the couple must reestablish the relationship they had before the children came along, and before the cares of life came in and pushed aside their primary relationship. The first step is to restore the "focus." Give your spouse an exclusive, concentrated place in your thoughts, ideas, and plans.

Don't be afraid to once again let him or her look into your soul as you once did when you both shared special, private dreams and ideas. At one time you shared things you were afraid to let the rest of the world in on. Your spouse had the "inside track" to your thoughts and your time. People aren't ashamed to seek the "inside track" in business, church, society, and government. But this focus and attention should be rightfully reserved for your lover.

DISCOVERY IN COURTSHIP

Second in the list of courtship qualities is discovery. In the early stages of courtship, there is much to learn about each other—preferences of foods, places to go, books, irritations, and favorite things to do. And truthfully, in the early years of courtship, the emphasis remains pretty much on sexual discovery and all the psychological and personal discoveries that are learned through this complicated new area of life exploration.

A man once told me, "It took me seven years to discover my wife's head. I became familiar with most of her body on our honeymoon, but we were married about seven years before I discovered that she had a mind." The man's statement is sad, but all too typical. He—and legions like him—know how to stimulate and satisfy a woman's body to bring her pleasure. But he never found out what his wife wanted, what she feared, what she dreamed about, what she hoped for. Those intimate and important matters were to remain hidden areas of life.

After a few years of marriage, many (if not all) of the couple's sexual and physiological discoveries have been made. But part of the relationship can remain stunted, unexplored, and unfulfilled. This undeveloped portion of the courtship has to do with learning about the hidden areas of life—areas not yet entrusted to another person. Every marriage has them, and if they have never come to light, a married couple should attempt to discover them as soon as possible. As these areas are revealed, the couple will confirm that the discovery process is continual.

During courtship we are obsessed to find new information about our lover. Likewise, as we attempt to restore courtship after marriage, we should be just as involved in this discovery process. Once again we should talk about the hidden areas, the secret fantasies, fears, dreams, and things that threaten to be too embarrassing to share with each other. Indeed, during this process, some people discover what many have called "the sanctity of the soul." This is an area, a hidden place, that we don't tell anyone about—not even a spouse.

Courtship in mature marriage allows the spouse entrance to even this remote area of sanctity, and gives the other person a glimpse of our own "inner sanctum" of true self and motives. Knowing one's partner from these deep recesses enhances the relationship to an extent that cannot be fully described. It's almost mystical. Perhaps this gives us better insight into the Hebrew word for sexual intercourse in the Bible, interpreted "to know."

GIVING IN COURTSHIP

Courtships are also characterized by giving. We give out of sheer joy—buying a present, wrapping it, and offering it as a symbol of love. I remember buying Janie's engagement ring. I had very little money and only a part-time job. I remember going to the jeweler to select the right ring. I soon learned that jewelers really understand young men in love, because I gave him a small down payment and he gave me a payment book. Each week I came in and made a payment. The jeweler marked down in my book how much I had paid. He provided terms so that after I had paid a certain amount, I could actually take the ring and give it to my fianceé.

Even now, decades later, I can remember the sheer joy on payday of walking to that jewelry store to hand them my $4 payment toward the engagement ring. I felt tremendous excitement as I eventually took the tiny, velvet-lined, spring-loaded box into my hand. I carefully double-checked to be sure the ring would not fall out, and I put the box in my pocket. Then I tried to come up with a romantic way to give it to Janie as an extension of myself so that she would understand my love.

A regular pattern of giving must exist in a mature marriage courtship. Do we hear the cues when a spouse mentions some desire to which we might respond with an unexpected gift? And if the gift doesn't seem to be practical, so what? Sometimes the effectiveness of a gift is directly proportional to how nonessential it is. Courtship responds to the desire of the heart, and is eager to supply that "special something" the other person would probably not buy for himself or herself. Such gifts that come from the heart are extensions of ourselves. That's why love letters mean so much during early courtship. Most poems and love letters are not great literature, but they are unmatched as gifts when we offer them to the one we love.

Occasionally you meet a couple who take pride in their practicality. When the man buys his wife a gift, it's likely to be a new frying pan that she needs. I once met a farmer who told me he was saving his money to buy his wife an egg washer, because one of her chores on their poultry farm was washing eggs. I'm sure the egg washer was a good and practical gift, but it occurred to me that the woman might have preferred some candy or flowers. A love poem might have been especially well-received in this instance, because for a practical economist, poems are quite cost effective!

I am a great believer in the division of labor in marriage. Certain tasks around our home are associated with Janie's life and other chores are mine. I put up storm windows, mow the lawn, dig holes, paint gutters, and generally do all of the outdoor chores. Janie's kitchen is hers. She doesn't even want me puttering around in it, especially when I make a mess.

On the other hand, our chores can provide us with wonderful opportunities to demonstrate love for each other. If I see that she's bogged down with too much other activity, I can sneak into the kitchen and do the dishes. Or sometimes when I'm unusually busy at work, I come home and find the lawn already mowed. Janie did something for me that she didn't have to do, something that wasn't on her list. But she did it anyway. And her actions say to me, "I love you. I know you are tired, and I wanted to help you." Such expressions are genuinely rich and satisfying for a couple.

In order for this system to work, however, you need to know whose work is whose. If each person is expecting the other to do a chore anyway, there are no special feelings when it gets done. Although the work might have been done as an expression of love, it won't necessarily be perceived as such.

Nevertheless, giving is part of the love-courtship process. It would be very wise, I think, for marriage partners to consider giving to each other in joyous ways. They should avoid the overly practical gifts that say, "Here's a way to help you do your job better." Instead, they should give those trivial, little things that express, "This is for no special reason other than to show you that I love you supremely."

SURPRISE IN COURTSHIP

Another part of youthful courtship is surprise. Do you remember doing things that your lover did not expect? The element of surprise is a wonderful part of blooming romances.

Maribelle Morgan wrote a marriage book a few years ago called *The Total Woman* (Fleming Revell), and she received criticism for some of the surprises she suggested in it. As a family friend, I find Charlie and Maribelle to be wonderful Christian people. Her book offered advice for improving the quality of a woman's married life by suggesting a lot of creative, innovative ideas. A few of them drew raised eyebrows from some Christians.

For example, one of her suggestions was for the woman to wrap her nude body in cellophane and wait for her husband to come home at the end of the day. Upon his arrival, she should throw open the door and say, "Surprise!" Some people laughed at this. Certain ministers preached against it. Others ridiculed it. But having known a few thousand men in my day, I would guess that virtually every husband would welcome such a treat—including those who laughed, scoffed, preached, or used other kinds of high-sounding arguments! I know hardly a man who wouldn't be turned on, excited, and delightfully happy that his wife playfully surprised him by offering herself to him in such a fresh, new, and abandoned way.

Maribelle's book offered a number of such surprises. You don't have to go with her ideas. But you can turn to your own ingenuity and creativity to restore the flavor, surprise, and excitement to your marriage.

As many people grow older, they learn to live without salt in their diet. I suppose it's a good idea from a health perspective. But life itself ought to have some spice. Everyone needs times of unexpected "seasoning" that make the blandness of daily life disappear. Such surprises ought to be something that every married person focuses on continually.

SPONTANEITY IN COURTSHIP

Closely akin to the concept of surprise is the need for spontaneity. Courtship involves doing unexpected things on the spur of the moment. Sometimes couples find themselves doing something that doesn't quite make sense or fit the plan—something out of the routine. Spontaneity can create fun and excitement out of an ordinarily humdrum, tedious relationship. Few things in marriage are as good as the times when we boldly say, "Let's do it! Let's give it a try." Special times happen when one person gets a fresh idea, communicates it with an excited sparkle in the eyes, and the other person says, "Sure! Why not? It might be fun."

Spontaneous activities might include a new experience, a new place to visit, or a new type of food to try. Or couples can find new ways of arranging their day and spending an evening. These spontaneous events make marriage more fun and exciting by helping eliminate the blahs and boredom.

On a large scale, I think spontaneity is the key to the enthusiasm so many people have for sports. We enjoy cheering for our teams because there is no way to predict with certainty how the event will turn out. On any given day, an innumerable number of things can happen to influence the outcome.

As a matter of fact, if sports events were totally predictable, they wouldn't be exciting at all. But athletic competition provides vivid spontaneity. An extra inch here, an unexpected call there, and the game demands your attention. Husbands and wives should see the parallel. Spontaneity adds excitement to marriage as well.

ADVENTURE IN COURTSHIP

Closely tied to spontaneity is the idea of adventure, which involves blending different kinds of experiences into a courtship. As a person approaches marriage, he or she has gone through a specific chain of events that has provided a unique experience. Courtship is the time for each person to share his or her experiences. Understanding each other's experiences is important during this time.

Courtship is enhanced by sharing experiences that have not taken place in either person's life so far, but that the couple can do together. Times away together, sharing new experiences, will help bind marriage partners in unity. These adventures can enrich our shared life and make it memorable.

I have a good friend who planned a raft trip for he and his wife down the Colorado River. They were to be gone for nearly a month. When I heard about it I thought, *What an extravagant use of time and money! Could I possibly take three weeks like that with Janie? Would she even be interested in going on a raft trip down the Colorado River?*

But later as we discussed their plans with them, we discovered they weren't really concerned about the adventure of rafting on the Colorado River as much as the adventure of restoring the zip, joy, and excitement of their marriage. Terrific! Theirs was to be the adventure of having something exclusive, something that would make their courtship special, new, and filled with zest.

Courtship ought to have many adventures like these that belong just to the couple. Some might involve risk.

Some might involve sacrifice of time or individual plans. Some might involve financial extravagance. But the benefits of these adventure experiences—the rekindling and restoration of courtship—far outweigh the costs.

ROMANCE IN COURTSHIP

Another powerful word that may describe the whole process of courtship is romance. This involves the unique mystery of the sexual relationship between man and woman—the chemistry which attracts males and females to each other. It's the special quality of love that causes a man to "leave his father and mother and cleave to his own wife."

Romance involves more than sexual technique. It has to do with the development of a special, private life-style of caring gestures, communication skills, and shared intimacies. Romance requires preparation. It might even involve inconvenience—going out of your way for a mate.

Romance is the impractical language of love. People who are not in love, nor ever have been, are easily embarrassed by romantic poetry. Even those of us who *have* been in love often find another writer's romantic expression too intimate to listen to in public. A certain song may be special to a couple when they are alone, but not when one of them happens to hear it on an elevator. Romance is surely a mystery.

The Bible speaks of "the way of a man with a maid" as being one of life's incomprehensible things. It is as complicated—and as poetic—as a bird moving through the air. It is fascinating to observe how universally God has built into His creation the attraction of the male to the female.

Even in the animal world we see the plumage, the courtship rituals and dances, the midair aerial acrobatics of the birds, and the fierce competition between males for mates. All these things indicate something magnificent about God's creation. Such an intricate, complex phenomenon should not be taken for granted by couples.

In fact, the mystery of romance is what God intended. Christian couples ought to have a better understanding of romance than secular people who have been brought up with self-centered approaches to romance, sex, and marriage. A careful reading of The Song of Solomon will help you discover the beauty of romance that should be part of the interpersonal vocabulary of men and women in love.

REKINDLING COURTSHIP

A courtship *can* be restored. And it *must* be restored if marriages are to avoid the common pitfalls.

I find it fascinating how the habits and relationships of courtship previously described reflect the fruit of the Spirit as listed in Scripture: love, joy, peace, patience, kindness, goodness, faithfulness, gentleness, and self-control (Galatians 5:22, 23). No one could ever come up with a better list of desired goals for courtship. The consistent application of these practical words is also encouraged in I Corinthians 13, a passage so often quoted during weddings.

The restoration of courtship and romance is a very practical need for any marriage—especially one that is experiencing turbulence. But beyond the practical application is a spiritual one: courtship (love) is actually a form of Christian worship.

We worship God by consistently relating to our fellow humans in the manner that He has prescribed in His Word. Christ's example and teaching provide a model for the way God wants us to love each other. For the Christian, restored courtship allows Christian faith to guide actions in the marriage relationship. But before this can successfully take place, the person must decide to do so through an act of the will. Each partner in marriage must commit to behave in a certain special manner toward the other person.

God doesn't command us to have romantic feelings and emotions for each other, but He does command us to love one another. And through the process of obedience to Him, a restored courtship can be rekindled.

Often it is the determined resolve of one marriage partner to love the other one that keeps the relationship from the abyss of marital breakup. Sometimes the determination to restore a courtship can prevent something just as bad as divorce—that dry, empty relationship that occurs when both people give up on the marriage and begin to live for themselves. Perhaps you've heard the old saying, "A person all wrapped up in himself (or herself) is a small package."

Why not try to spark a new romantic courtship adventure? Review the elements listed in this chapter and apply them in your own special way. The experiences that so excited and electrified your courtship and early married life are guaranteed to work again—as soon as somebody begins to act on them.

CHAPTER NINE

The Rediscovery Process

Following the restoration of courtship, a couple should feel the need for a rediscovery process. Courtship is simply the prelude—a time for establishing proper attitudes and setting the groundwork for the serious business of rediscovery in marriage. Though courtship itself contains a significant amount of discovery, such discovery often gets interrupted by things that creep into daily life. And when the discovery process becomes interrupted, postponed, or neglected, the stage is set for tedium and taking one another for granted.

We know this to be true on a spiritual level. In regard to their relationships with Jesus, Christians are admonished to endure hardship as soldiers—not becoming entangled with the cares or affairs of this life (II Timothy 2:3, 4). Yet on a personal level, we lower our guard and allow those same concerns of life to detract us and prevent us from pleasing a spouse.

Another potential distraction from harmony with a spouse is vocation. If vocational pursuits are not shared, they can interrupt the discovery of each other. Often as young marrieds, self-esteem is not very well formed. We may try to build it through vocational and career positioning, hoping for a sense of fullness. But we've already discussed how this preoccupation with career goals can separate us from the ones we love most.

Other legitimate goals (house, car, children, social club, or even church) can also drive a wedge into our marriage relationships if we aren't careful. Part of the rediscovery process is to isolate such things that may have become the enemies of growth together. The marriage relationship can be restored by rediscovering one another at a new, more mature stage, after putting all the other goals into proper perspective.

'Is That Really Me?'

Have you ever gone back to a high school or family reunion and "rediscovered" someone you haven't seen in years? Often the most outstanding quality that comes out of that meeting is the solid impression of how much the person has changed. (No doubt the other person feels the same about you.) But within a marriage, we often miss this growth because it takes place in such small ways over a long period of time.

Occasionally you may browse through home movies, old letters, or photograph albums. As you look at yourself as you were ten or more years ago, you ask, "Do I know that person? Is that really me?" The truth of the matter is, no. That person is not really you. Through life's growth experiences, you have attained a different level of maturity—one, it is hoped, that is deeper and more profound. The same is true of your spouse.

It's one thing for you to rediscover yourself in this process. But beyond that, you need to review your years of marriage and ponder, "Who is this person to whom I am married? And how can I strengthen my relationship to this person?"

A nightclub ballad speaks of love "the second time around." The inference is that if you give up on your first marriage, take hope because you'll be a wiser person during the next one. The song suggests that the second marriage will have depth that the first one didn't, and I suppose the logic of such a statement can be true. But is it necessary to throw away a marriage to achieve that deeper level of success?

My point is, "Why not try to find love the second time around *with the same person*?" It's much less complicated. You've already invested so much of yourself in your present marriage. You have spent enormous effort learning about each other and getting where you are. Why give up that foundation to start again from scratch?

THE SOCIAL EXCHANGE THEORY

If a person wanted to analyze this on a strictly scientific basis, he could use something called the Social Exchange Theory. By using a simple formula, a person can measure the cost of marriage against the rewards of marriage. Simply put, you list all the short-term and long-term costs that you put into your marriage—time, money, adjustments, arguments, sacrifices, etc. Then you list the rewards—companionship, sexual pleasure, shared experiences, children, happiness, and growth.

The Social Exchange Theory will usually indicate that the rewards of marriage are worth the costs. But even when there is doubt on this point, the same formula can be used to forecast what might happen if you ended the marriage.

What are the costs of divorce in terms of suffering, financial hardship, child custody matters, social stigma, spiritual disobedience, and so forth? Write out that list and weigh it against your expected rewards. Do you have any guarantee that a new marriage will work any better? Can you be sure that love will be better "the second time around"?

I believe there have been enough studies done to tell us that marriage is often far worse the second time. So why not redeem what already exists rather than throw it aside? Even if you have learned certain lessons with one person, it won't be likely that you can apply them to someone else. This other person's experience won't be the same as that of your present spouse. It will be far easier and potentially more successful for you and your spouse to try again—together.

The Christian should have an advantage in this rediscovery process. Christianity involves a deep and unique understanding of grace, the quality of forgiveness that involves both forgetting past grievances and restoration of fellowship. As we first experience the all-encompassing level of Christ's forgiveness, then we begin to understand that nothing in our marriage is beyond redemption.

WHAT HAVE WE LEARNED?

For the Christian who desires to save a marriage, there is a process that can make all the difference. Let me suggest four steps of rediscovery that provide a way to start all over again as two brand-new persons.

The first step has to do with lessons already learned. Both partners in marriage need a willingness to admit that they were unrealistic in their early expectations. In the initial period of marriage, both partners are usually guilty of being unfair. They both need to confess that they came into their marriage with more "baggage" than they had estimated.

Many people don't realize just how much their backgrounds affect them, even with small things. A recent "Dear Abby" letter was sent by a husband who had been taught to clean his plate at every meal. His wife was raised in a well-to-do home where it was considered poor manners to eat everything on the plate. This couple's marriage was in trouble because of these backgrounds.

No doubt you have your own stories to tell, so it is important to take some time to make a list of lessons learned. Your list doesn't have to be as sophisticated as a Social Exchange Theory. Perhaps all it will take is a legal pad with columns to record unrealistic expectations, unreasonable demands, underestimated baggage, and specific examples of times when you were unfair. Ask yourself: "What have I learned together about my marriage so far? What have been my mistakes?" Then take your whole page full of experience and title it "Lessons Learned."

Together, with your marriage partner, prayerfully present your lists to God and ask for forgiveness, realizing that there are two sides to every story. Your past problems may be too complex to truly straighten out at this point. So why not simply bring them to the cross and say, "Dear God, we want to start over again. We want this marriage restored. We want to rediscover who we are. We admit that both of us have made mistakes and have said some things we shouldn't have, but we are wiser now. We want You, God, to wipe the slate clean. We want to start over with these lessons learned." (Even if one partner is primarily responsible for a major error or sin, both parties should seek forgiveness and restoration.)

I have often called this my pearl theory. Do you know how an oyster behaves when it gets a jagged piece of foreign material inside its shell? Using fluids from its own body, the oyster surrounds that painful annoyance layer by layer, and eventually turns it into a pearl.

Our painful marriage experiences can also become "pearls" when we allow God, through His grace, to take our sins, mistakes, misgivings, misunderstandings, and failings, and to surround them with His love and forgiveness. In the process, He also takes away the naivety and foolishness of our early misconceptions. He turns those annoyances into lessons for personal growth to be used for the rest of our lives.

WHO ARE WE NOW?

The second of the four steps is to consider the question, "Who are we now?" Very likely you are not as naive as you were when you first married, but you're not as confident either. Your experiences have left you a little afraid. You feel some anger over missed opportunities. Even though you may have grown, there were dues to pay—and those costs may have left you feeling resentful.

So when was the last time you and your partner sat down to discuss with each other what kind of people you have become? Have the two of you taken inventory as to how and where each has grown? Are you committed to seeing it through together?

Take time to talk about where you are now. Share with each other what you have learned about life and its positive/negative experiences over the years you've been married. Think back to who and what you were when you first met. Discuss what you hoped for versus what you have become in each area of your life. You'll discover that neither of you is exactly the same as when you began the relationship. And because both of you have changed, you can now build on a new foundation.

Remember, as Christians we need to affirm each other. As we see each other change, we should remember that every person is of value. It's okay to share what you feel are areas for the other's improvement, but do not do so at the expense of that person's self-esteem. Build the other person up. Make him or her feel welcome to be the person he or she is. And before long, you begin to develop mutual trust.

Your conversations will demonstrate that the two of you are infinitely more experienced and wiser, and that you probably will not make the same mistakes. You have learned something about the principle of "give-and-take." In order for the two to more easily become one, you are now ready to adapt, adjust, and compromise.

"Who are we *now*?" is an important question to ask. Other questions are unproductive and even harmful: Such questions to avoid are: "What were we?" "What happened?" "Who made the most mistakes?" "Who failed?" "Who is guilty?" Ask instead: "Who are these two people looking at each other across the kitchen table?" "Based on experiences shared over a period of years, how can they now start over?" "What can they do to begin a new courtship process to really love one another?"

WHERE DOES GOD FIT INTO OUR RELATIONSHIP?

A third necessary step in the rediscovery process is consideration of the question: "How does God fit into our relationship?" I think the answer is evident. We can't submit to each other until we have submitted to God. Yet a lot of people struggle with the idea of submission, working under a terrible misconception that turning over our freedom to God means the end of individual creativity and spontaneity. Some people feel that submission causes them to be domesticated to such a degree that life no longer holds any excitement.

This is a foolish and faulty understanding of freedom. Living simply to satisfy our appetites and desires—what we want, when we want it—is the worst kind of slavery. Such attitudes make us captive to our appetites and emotions. To be really free is to be yielded to someone else—to "belong" to that other person. And giving one's life over to God is the beginning of freedom.

A wild dog is free, but it is almost always infested with parasites. He eats whatever he finds, but you can count all the ribs along his sides. He may have had part of his ear torn off in a fight. And as he lives free, he will also die free—most likely from being ravaged by a larger animal, freezing, starving, or dying of thirst.

On the other hand, the domesticated dog is submissive to a master. He is combed, cared for, groomed, and made beautiful. He is stronger, weighs more, and has more contentment. The domesticated dog enjoys his walks with his master. It doesn't have to kill to eat. Its food is lovingly prepared by his owner.

Do you see the analogy? It is only when we allow God through His Word to "domesticate" us that we can realize our full potential. When we willingly live within the boundaries of His designs for our life, we find freedom!

As marriage partners, a major step in the rediscovery and rebuilding process is including God in your lives in a brand-new way. As a measure of the act of salvation, you have given your lives over to God. Now, together, you need to give your lives (as a couple) over to Christ in obedience to His purposes and commands.

I often draw this picture for couples:

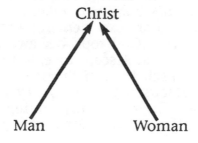

Notice that the closer each person gets to Christ, the closer he or she also gets to the other person. This is exactly the way it works in our marriage relationship. Drawing near to God automatically (and naturally) brings us closer to our marriage partners. Our hearts, minds, motives, and desires become closer to the other person's because we have the common goal of Christlikeness.

We may occasionally forget that marriage is God's idea and part of His divine plan. God brings couples together and knows how to "fix" relationships when marriages go sour. In fact, the only permanent solution for failing marriages is to come together and truly allow God to become central in this rediscovered partnership between two people who are now wiser and more mature.

WHAT ARE OUR PLANS FOR THE FUTURE?

The fourth step of the process involves plans for the future. One of my most favorite books written to Christians on this subject is *A Severe Mercy* (Sheldon Vanauken, Harper and Row). This skillfully written and highly moving book is about the author and his lover as they entered marriage. Sheldon and his young wife became totally immersed in each other. They both had a loving commitment and loyalty for the other. Each one desired a lifetime marriage based on the same kinds of values that young lovers begin with—a kind of perpetual Romeo and Juliet idealized love.

But the wife died at a young age from a terminal illness. Her love-obsessed husband became bitter because the love of his life had been snatched away. Sheldon questioned his friend, author C. S. Lewis, about this problem. Lewis responded with a letter from which the title of Vanauken's book was taken. In essence, Lewis wrote: "Maybe you are experiencing a severe mercy. The severe mercy is that God took her away, lest you spend your entire lives in adolescent love, lest your marriage be preoccupied with self and selfish concerns."

For those discussing rediscovery in marriage and beginning a new life together, planning for the future is considerably different than for a young couple looking into each other's eyes and discovering each other for the first time. The "seasoned" couple sees life more realistically because of the maturity that comes through years of difficulties, failures, and triumphs. They are still concerned about goals for the future. But they also want to know practical things, such as how children (even grandchildren) should affect their relationship, or how to handle parents for whom they have responsibility.

Mature discussion is the mark of a truly rediscovered marriage. The husband and wife will not revert to adolescent attitudes, but will instead reestablish the relationship around new activities while making room for service. And this time the discussion will involve plans for each individual's (as well as the couple's) growth.

A FRIGHTENING IDEA

Some people might question the necessity of growing. Sometimes the attitude is, "I already know what I need to know. I've learned what it takes to get along in the world." But a Christian understands that there is a life to come, and that we are always growing toward that future level of perfection.

If you stopped learning, discovering, or deepening your life and relationships sometime in your early twenties, would you be content to stay at that level forever? I think most people would find this to be a frightening idea. I wonder, then, why people would be satisfied in a marriage that covers forty, fifty, or sixty years, without any growth.

Jesus spoke about marriage in the context of eternity. He said, "At the resurrection people will neither marry nor be given in marriage" (Matthew 22:30). I think His comments were directed to the concepts of procreation, sexuality, sperm and ovum, and the aspect of male and female. Since we are created in the image of God, I believe when we arrive in eternity we will enjoy a time of never-ending individual creative endeavor. So as preparation for that worthwhile activity, we should make sure that our marriages continue to mature throughout our 50th anniversaries, or however long we are together.

We can experience great happiness on earth when our rediscovered marriages are strengthened by the lessons we have learned. Think of the pleasure, joy, and satisfaction to find yourself learning and growing right up to the very end of your existence on this earth, after which you are able to present to God a life that is as fully developed as possible. Together, through your marriage, you and your spouse can become one in the fullest sense.

CHAPTER TEN

A New Intimacy: Two Shall Become One

The goal of marriage is for two people to become one. That fact underscores the reality that couples *do* begin a marriage as two separate beings. They are two different people with different backgrounds, different genders, different experiences, different prejudices, and different ideas about the future. Perhaps they even have different values.

Yet those two completely different people commit to a relationship where they are asked to blend their differences. And as they continue to work toward their commitment, they eventually reach the point where "they are no longer two, but one" (Matthew 19:6).

Interestingly, the language of the Bible is rather precise from both a sociological and psychological viewpoint. Sociologically, each individual is a separate person—very different from all others. Certain tests could bear out just *how* different. In a physical sense, two people can become one through sexual intercourse which gives psychological union. Yet the new intimacy of two people becoming one is actually a process which takes a lifetime to achieve. Two people do not become one at marriage ceremony simply because a pastor says so. Nor do they truly become one when their two bodies are joined in the bedroom on the wedding night.

None of these considerations are going through the minds of young couples as they stand at the wedding altar. They are caught up in the vows, ceremony, reception, opening the gifts, that wild ride to the hotel, the slow ride up the elevator, and the intense consummation of the marriage during the honeymoon. These concerns are important and good, but they are only the prelude to the process of creating a new intimacy.

OVERCOMING THE FEARS OF BECOMING ONE

God intends that we become one in a different, deeper, lasting, and more meaningful way. We enter marriage with deep fears and hidden secrets, but the wonderful truth is that we can eventually achieve victory over fear.

One common fear is the loss of modesty when each partner sees the other for the first time without the usual coverings. Nakedness is one concern, but so is the matter of allowing the other person to see us without the "right" clothes and trappings that supposedly give us class, beauty, or virility.

For the first time, we are "exposed" to the other person for 24 hours a day, and during part of that time we will not look our best. But with time and experience, this fear of exposure disappears. We finally become comfortable sharing the truth of our physical appearances with another human being.

Yet conquering this fear of rejection is only a beginning. The unclothing of the body is nothing compared to what it takes to bare the mind and the soul. The goal of becoming one is *complete* transparency, including being at ease as we share our most tentative ideas and expose our emotions for the other person to see. One of the most important goals of marriage is to eliminate the fear that prevents this kind of oneness.

The Bible tells us that, "Perfect love drives out fear" (I John 4:18). Fear involves anticipated judgment or punishment. So it is a marvelous accomplishment for God to guide us into a relationship with another human being where fear of judgment, rejection, and embarrassment can eventually be eliminated.

A MATTER OF TOLERANCE

This process of two people becoming one also involves the development of tolerance, which is a result of diversity. Single people may get by with judging people and events based solely on how those things relate to them personally. But a married couple responds from a oneness that provides a more realistic view of life and the world.

The person who expects diversity between human beings sees life from the other's point of view and benefits from such a perspective. Great wisdom and experience is available from truly loving and yielding to another human being who is so different from yourself—someone whose ideas, values, dreams, goals, and ambitions are entirely different from your own. As you learn to deal with diversity, you develop tolerance and respect for the other person.

It is at this point that maturity begins. Immature people cannot handle diversity of any kind. But as people mature, they discover that the world is made up of these differences and that diversity is actually part of the treasure of God's vast and complex creation.

These truths are part of the new intimacy husbands and wives experience with each other within a marriage. They also help couples develop an intimacy in other relationships as they become more tolerant of diversity.

A CRAVING FOR COMPANIONSHIP

Still another result of oneness in marriage is the essential element of companionship. We were created by God to love and to serve one another.

Have you ever observed an older person who has a special companionship with a pet? They think about it all the time and care for it constantly. They buy special treats, toys, and sweaters as they dote over it. Interestingly, psychologists tell us that people who have the companionship of a cat or dog actually live longer than people who don't.

What a fascinating (yet incomplete) illustration of truth. If, in fact, love for an animal can have such an effect on people, how much greater must be the benefits of human companionship to enrich and prolong life! Human companionship returns the love, loyalty, and trust that is invested in the relationship. And in the context of marriage, there are the further benefits of intellectual and sexual stimulation. Humans should not be evaluated as a little higher than animals; we are actually just a little lower than the angels (Psalm 8:5).

There is almost an infinite difference between the benefits of living with a pet and the satisfaction of interacting with another human being. Likewise, the marvelous relationship we can have with God is infinitely greater than any relationship we might have with another human being—no matter how good. The new intimacy of marriage gives us a better understanding of the full richness of companionship and love available to human beings.

In fact, it is only through marriage that we can begin to glimpse the benefits available when we commit to developing a closer relationship with God. As we begin to reveal our real (otherwise hidden) personalities, we discover that God accepts us as we are. As we mold our wills and goals to those He has for us, we discover a deeper bond than we ever could have imagined.

This is not to say that unmarried people can never understand God. A sensitive single person who reads widely, thinks deeply, and is caring and observant can learn much more than a married person who is selfish, totally insensitive, or a bore. Yet if two people in marriage really become one in the sense that God intends, the experience can't help but refine their understanding of God. A healthy marriage tends to make spiritual life all the more richer.

GOD'S MASTER PLAN

God could have created the human race as a group of autonomous individuals. He didn't have to require a man and woman to enter into a relationship of sexuality, mutual care, and loyalty over a long period of time. He could even have caused children to be created as they do in science fiction films—through clones, cocoons, or an InstaKid pill dropped into water.

Our omnipotent God had millions of possibilities as He designed humankind. But He chose to do it the way He has for a special reason. I believe that reason, at its deepest level, is to not only help us discover more about each other through marriage, but also to give us a better understanding of Him.

As God approached the creation of people, we are told, "Male and female He created them" (Genesis 1:27). In His wisdom He created two distinct genders, each with its own strengths and weaknesses. Neither is ever truly complete without the other. Yet we know that God's creation came out of His own completeness. So we must conclude that there are some things about God's nature that the male can never know until he has developed a caring and responsible relationship with a female. And there are things that a female will never discover about God until she experiences a relationship with a loving, sensitive male.

It is not too presumptuous to suggest that within the marriage relationship, the mysteries of the universe are hidden. Christ is the Bridegroom and we, as the Church, are His bride. This is more than a simple illustration. It is an extension of reality. Christ actually is the Bridegroom and the Church really is the bride. God is actually our Father and we are really His sons and daughters.

As we come to understand these truths, the depth of God's relationship to all mankind is revealed to us. It also provides us with a new outlook as we interact with other people. When we feel the pain of estrangement or divorce, we sense something of what God must feel when His "bride" separates herself from Him. When our hearts go out to loved ones facing crises of different kinds, we better understand the compassion God has for us as a Father for His children. When we undergo the pain of someone's infidelity to us, we more fully appreciate God's continual loving care and faithfulness.

God does care about us. He does understand our feelings. But sometimes we don't truly comprehend these facts until we go through negative experiences and severe hurts.

DON'T GIVE UP THE (RELATION)SHIP

In summary, the purpose of two people becoming one is not simply to carry on romance or procreation. Rather, we become one so we can more fully understand God's nature and draw closer to Him. Even as imperfect human beings, we need to be preparing for the day when we will live with God for all eternity.

I am convinced that your marriage relationship should not be abandoned so easily. The divorce statistics that we read about today are not simply broken marriage contracts. They are really broken covenants with God.

A contract is an important document, but it is still less binding than a covenant. A covenant is a promise made to God. The commitment to live together in a marriage relationship is not only a contract between two people, but also a covenant between each of those people and God. And according to the apostle John, we prove that we love God by showing love for each other (I John 4:20).

This is my central point. In marriage, you agree to a pact that involves loving one another, caring for one another, nurturing one another, and faithfulness to one another. You vow to see the marriage through—in sickness or health, for richer or poorer, and forsaking all others. Do you not see that it is exactly this kind of relationship that God wants to have with you? God is a supremely faithful bridegroom who will never be guilty of infidelity. He will never abandon you (Joshua 1:5). He is your constant companion for facing difficulty (Psalm 46:1). God understands you at your deepest level, aware of your darkest secrets and glaring failures, yet still desiring to maintain a relationship with you.

Such faithfulness is beyond what most of us can even imagine. Yet God gave us marriage as a picture of this wonderful "forever" relationship.

So is your marriage worth fighting for? Absolutely! Are outside forces trying to break it up? Absolutely!

Satan's efforts are focused against marriage as he tries to destroy this relationship that can bring you such happiness, joy, and spiritual growth. Can a fractured and broken marriage be restored? Absolutely! It may not be easy, but it is certainly possible.

In order for the restoration process to succeed, the couple needs to be willing to apply the same degrees of Christian discipleship, obedience, and commitment to their marriage that they give to their eternal salvation. Just as they yielded to God when they received Christ as Savior, each partner must once again yield his or her will—this time to the other person.

Can you make such a commitment of will to make your marriage work? The decision is yours. Can your courtship be restored? Without question! It will happen when two caring, intelligent people make daily choices to do so. Love is behavior, and it is possible to restore love by acting in obedience to God.

Can couples claim a new relationship? Yes—if they refuse to give up and agree to try harder.

Every marriage is likely to go through the stages that have been discussed in this book, starting at the level of immaturity. Only those who commit to trying harder will survive. It's not unlike a runner who has to persevere to win the race. Marriage requires the same perseverance. The rewards are all in front of you. But you will only stand victorious at the finish line if you commit your marriage and your will to God by repeatedly saying, "I refuse to give up on this. I *will* make it work."

This book has been written with the prayer and deep desire that couples who are Christians—those who are truly serious about their relationship with God—will not allow themselves to fail in this effort. It's much too easy to fall into the statistical traps that typify modern culture. But if you are a Christian, you can be sure that faith in the same God who saved your eternal soul will also save your marriage from damnation and destruction.

Is it possible? Absolutely!